THE RISE OF A WINNER
CRISTIANO
RONALDO

This book is dedicated to the author's sister and brother, Tana and Brian, and to Patrick Hasburgh, for his mentoring and inspiration.
A special thank you to Yonatan Ginsberg for his contribution to this book.
His love and depth of knowledge of the beautiful game were invaluable.

Also by Michael Part

The Flea: The Amazing Story of Leo Messi

Neymar The Wizard

Balotelli: The Untold Story

James: The Incredible Number 10

Luis Suarez: A Striker's Story

THE RISE OF A WINNER
CRISTIANO RONALDO

MICHAEL PART

Sole
BOOKS

Published by Sole Books Beverly Hills
www.solebooks.com

A special thank you to Yonatan Ginsberg for his contribution
to this book. His love and depth of knowledge of the beautiful
game were invaluable. Special thanks to Yaron and Guy Ginsberg.

Series editor: Y Ginsberg
Front cover photo ©: AP Photo/Andres Kudacki
Back cover photo ©: REUTERS/Felix Ordonez
Cover design: Omer Pikarski
Page layout: Lynn Snyder

ISBN: 978-1-938591-55-6
E-ISBN: 978-1-938591-56-3

Library of Congress Cataloging-in-Publication data available
Join Cristiano Ronaldo The Rise of a Winner on Facebook

CHAPTER 1

Cristiano Ronaldo dos Santos Aveiro splashed some water on his face. He stared at himself in the mirror and made a face. He took a deep breath. This was his day.

Outside, on the Paseo de la Castellana in Madrid, heavy traffic pulsated past the Santiago Bernabéu Stadium. It was 6 July 2009 and fans had waited hours to get a seat for the day's event. The 82,000 stadium seats filled up quickly. Those who did not get in watched the festivities on big screen monitors outside the stadium.

People were dressed in the white jerseys of FC Real Madrid. One of the world's best players was finally coming to their team.

The famous Real Madrid emblem decorated the front of his jersey, which hung in his locker, with his name and the number 9 stitched on the back. How long had he dreamt of this moment? He couldn't remember a time he hadn't dreamed about playing for Real Madrid. Growing up, he would say he wanted to play for Real Madrid and everyone would always say, 'Who doesn't?'

He looked around. The Bernabéu. He was finally here. A permanent smile on his face, Cristiano closed his eyes and took another deep breath. They would say his name over the loudspeakers and he would trot across the pitch to the stage. That's all there was to do. Climb the stairs, say what he had to say. Shake some hands and take some pictures. He was used to the cameras, but this was different. This was the dream of a lifetime coming true.

He worried that his nerves would get the better of him. He turned back to his new locker. Inside were a number of crucifixes. He had a whole collection of them, but these were his favourites. It was almost time to go.

The way to the pitch was down a set of stairs that led out of the team dressing room, through a short hall and up a blue steel staircase. As soon as he hit the hallway, he heard the crowd. When he got to the blue stairs, the sound was deafening. This was his debut and the powers-that-be at Real Madrid wanted it to be dramatic. From the bottom of the stairs, it sounded like everyone in Madrid was there.

He stayed in the shadows and took a final deep breath, then climbed the stairs like the rungs of a ladder. His heart raced when he spotted the greatest player Madrid had ever seen, Alfredo di Stefano, on stage. The Blonde Arrow! And right next to him, one of the best football players of all time – The Black Pearl himself: Eusébio – a legend in Portugal, who many compared to Pelé. There they were, his heroes, waiting for him. It was unreal.

He was just a poor kid who learned everything he knew about the beautiful game on the streets of Madeira. How did he get here? How did he get to the top of the world of football? He closed his eyes and saw the island of his childhood once more: the broken streets, the patchwork shanties, and the football pitches. He felt his childhood coming back to him. His first memory was a church. And he was wearing blue and white.

CHAPTER 2

Reverend Antonio Rodriguez Rebola glanced down
at his list of baptisms for the day. All the names
were crossed off but one. It had been a busy
afternoon at the Santo Antonio Church high on the
hill and the Aveiro baby, Cristiano Ronaldo, was the
last on his list. He wanted to go home. He looked
over at the mother, Maria Dolores Aveiro, her
children, and her sister, all seated on the wooden
bench near the font. The stoup was made of solid
marble and carved into the shape of an angel
holding an open seashell, filled with holy water.
Dolores' sister stuck two fingers into the font,
wet them, and playfully flicked them in Dolores'
face. The two women giggled. The baby, Cristiano
Ronaldo, was sound asleep.

Reverend Rebola lifted his sleeve and checked

his watch. The christening was to be at 6pm. It was already two minutes after 6 and Jose Dinis, the father, had not yet arrived. He did not see the godfather, Fernão de Sousa, either. Dolores felt the Reverend's gaze burning into her. She knew where her husband and the godfather were and she knew she could not do anything about it.

Not far from the church, in the Andorinha pitch, a game between Andorinha and Ribeiras Brava was about to end. Team Captain Jose Fernão Barros de Sousa, Cristiano's godfather, was already on the pitch. Jose Dinis, the baby's father, was the kit man for the team. He sat on the bench looking at his watch: they were already late to his son's baptism, but what could he do? The game started half an hour late. He hoped that the ref wouldn't add any extra time and he prayed to God the priest would wait.

Reverend Rebola approached Dolores. She could tell by his face that he was nervous so she smiled and tried to relax him.

'I hope your husband and the godfather are on their way.'

'They should be here any minute,' she said. She hoped the Reverend wouldn't ask why they were late. Not everyone on the island of Madeira was as obsessed with football as her family.

Dolores' sister looked over at her one-year-old nephew who was fast asleep. 'Cristiano is patient,' she said.

The Reverend heard the women talking and looked at the baby. 'You call him Cristiano?' he asked.

'His full name is Cristiano Ronaldo,' Dolores said proudly. 'Ronaldo. After Ronald Reagan.'

'The US president?' the Reverend asked.

'Yes, but before he was president he was a great actor,' Dolores said. 'And we like him a lot.'

The Reverend scratched his head. He knew that the US president was a movie star back before he became a politician.

Dolores smiled. 'We love all his films, they make us happy.'

The Reverend smiled too. 'Cristiano Ronaldo,' he said, musing. 'Future president? Or maybe even a movie star?'

The women giggled.

At precisely 6.30pm, Fernão's car screeched into the small dirt car park of the Santo Antonio church. Jose Dinis and Fernão got out and rushed inside, tightening their ties, pulling on their suit coats, and tucking in their white shirts over their blue and white Andorinha jerseys. Both men stopped at the door out of respect. Jose Dinis smoothed his hair, then linked arms with Fernão and led the way into the church.

The baptism of Cristiano Ronaldo dos Santos Aveiro went off without a hitch. Reverend Rebola was greatly relieved. Cristiano did not make a peep. When the christening was over, it was time for the photograph. Although Reverend Rebola fully expected Mr and Mrs Aveiro to dress the infant Cristiano in a baptism gown for this precious moment, he wasn't the least bit surprised when Jose Dinis insisted his son be photographed in the team colours of *Clube de Futebol Andorinha de Santo António.*

Dolores sat Cristiano down. She quickly pulled some white booties on him and she and her sister shoved gold bracelets on his wrists, a gold ring on his finger, and a crucifix around his neck.

The church photographer was ready to snap the shot. 'Ready?' he asked. 'One... two... three...!'

Cristiano Ronaldo turned his head to the camera with his dark eyes open wide and stared directly into the lens as if he had done it a thousand times. As if he knew what to do.

The photographer snapped the picture and everyone clapped.

CHAPTER 3

The Aveiro house was so small, Jose Dinis put the washing machine on the roof. He always said their laundry room had the best view in all of Madeira. Five-year-old Cristiano shared the house with his mother, Dolores; his father, Jose Dinis; his two sisters, Elma and Katia; and his brother, Hugo. They all lived in the hillside village of Santo Antonio in Funchal, the capital city of Madeira. Mum and dad shared one bedroom and the four children shared the other. The bedroom window was practically the only light in the tiny three-room home, except for the light that streamed in through the dozen or so holes in the ceiling. They didn't have enough money to fix it. The third room was where they got together as a family. There was also a bathroom, the size of a cupboard.

Cristiano sat on his porch and watched the boys march past his house and up the hill to Lombinho Street. He knew they were going to play football because one of them always had a ball tucked under his arm, and they all sported jerseys of their favourite teams. Rua Quinta Falcão, Hawk Farm Street, was steep. The kids who played out front were always chasing balls down the hill. They had to learn to be quick or they would find themselves halfway down the hill before they caught their ball. So the older boys liked to play up the hill at Caminho do Lombinho, just past the Maritimo football pitch, where it was flat.

Maritimo was a Primeira Liga team, one of the two best football teams on the island. It was Jose Dinis' favourite team. The other Primiera Liga team in Madeira was Nacional, which was his mother's favourite team. She was also a fan of Sporting Lisbon, one of the best clubs in Portugal. The Aveiro house was always tense every time there was a match between the two local clubs, known as the Madeira Derby. At five years old, Cristiano had already been to many matches with his father. Football meant everything to him.

Cristiano smelled his supper cooking inside and his stomach responded. The boys waved as they walked by. The boy with the ball dropped it to his foot and comfortably juggled it back up to his hands. Then he did it again.

Cristiano leapt to his feet. 'I want to play!' he shouted, running out into the street.

The boys just laughed. Adelino, the boy with the ball, pushed him back. 'You're too young!' he said. 'You gotta be at least six!' Another boy shouted and the rest of the boys laughed some more and their laughter faded as they charged up the hill.

Cristiano stomped back to his porch, disappointed, and kicked the wall. 'I'm not too young! I'm almost six!' he said and kicked the wall again. He thought about it for a moment, then sat down and took off his shoes and socks, and wadded up his socks into a ball. He stood up, dropped the sock-ball and caressed it with the top of his foot, launched it back up, and caught it in his fingertips. Just like the older boys. He did it a lot. He did it until it was perfect every time, even with his eyes closed.

He heard a whistle from behind him. He spun around. His father was just coming up the street from Andorinha. Jose Dinis waved, dropped his kit bag, and opened his arms wide like a giant eagle.

'Dad!' Cristiano shouted and charged down the hill to meet him. When he got there, he let his father engulf him with his arms. There was no greater feeling than when he wrapped himself in his father's arms. Jose Dinis held his youngest son tightly to his chest, then looked down at his son's bare feet.

'Where are your shoes?'

'On the porch,' Cristiano said, pointing back up the hill to their home.

'Playing ball with your socks again?' Jose Dinis asked, smiling.

Cristiano squeezed his father even tighter. 'I lost the ball you gave me,' he said. 'I kicked it too hard and it went down the hill.'

'Well, you're supposed to chase it!' His father said, smiling.

'I did!' Cristiano said. 'But it disappeared in the bushes. I think it went off the cliff and fell into the ocean.'

Jose Dinis laughed and undid his son's arms, then pulled open the drawstring on his kit bag, reached in, and produced a scuffed-up ball. 'For you,' he said solemnly, handing it over. 'This time try to hang on to it.'

Cristiano froze and his eyes grew wide. 'You got me a new ball,' he whispered reverently.

'Yes, like new, Cristiano,' his father said.

Cristiano turned the ball over in his hands, looking at every square inch of it. 'Is it really mine?'

'No, I got it for the kid down the road,' Jose Dinis said.

'What?!' Cristiano shouted and started crying.

Jose Dinis felt terrible. 'Stop! Cristiano! Don't cry. Come on,' he said, wrapping his arms around his son once more. 'I was just kidding!'

Cristiano looked up at his father and his eyes were wet with tears. He let out a sniffling chuckle and buried his face in his father's sweaty shirt, wiping his nose on it.

'Heyyyy!' Jose Dinis said when he saw what his son had done.

Cristiano giggled and charged off back up the hill to their home as Dolores came out onto the porch.

'Mum, look!' Cristiano shouted and showed her the ball his father had given him. She tried to take it from him and he pulled away. 'It's mine! Get your own!'

Dolores laughed. 'Well, let's eat dinner first! It's on the table getting cold!' Dolores said and scooted Cristiano into the house.

Cristiano put down his fork. 'I'm full.' Everyone looked at his plate, still piled with food. Dolores had made *bacalhau,* a traditional Portuguese dish consisting of salted cod, potatoes, and scrambled eggs. But they couldn't afford the cod this week, so it was *bacalhau* without the fish and even though Cristiano was just five, he knew when he was being fed a plateful of vegetables.

Jose Dinis sat at one end of the table and Dolores at the other. The four children sat around the table, two on each side. Cristiano sat next to his father.

'You're done?' Dolores asked, poker-faced, shooting a quick look to her husband.

Cristiano nodded enthusiastically. Under the table, his right foot kept his new ball in place.

'If you want to play,' Jose Dinis said, munching a forkful of food. 'You need energy. Energy does not come from the air, you know. It comes from eating your vegetables.'

'Eat two bites of potatoes and two bites of egg and drink all of your milk,' Dolores said.

Cristiano obeyed and spooned some eggs and potatoes into his mouth, then more eggs and potatoes. He knew how to count and knew what a *couple* meant and soon his cheeks bulged like a hamster. His mouth was so full he could barely chew.

Katia tried to hold back her laughter, but she could not help looking at her younger brother and every time she did, she laughed. And when she started laughing, so did Elma and Hugo. Dolores looked the other way and Jose Dinis just smiled. There was never a dull moment with this one, Jose Dinis thought.

'Okay. Go play,' he said.

By the time his father said 'go,' Cristiano was already out the door, ball in hand.

'Don't lose this one!' Jose Dinis said as he chased after his son. When he got to the street, Cristiano was already half a block up the hill, dribbling the ball first with his right foot, then his left. He had more speed than any five-year-old he had ever seen. And he had the moves down. Although they couldn't afford their own TV, the Aveiro family was always invited over to one neighbour's house or another to watch a match. It never failed, after a match, that Cristiano mastered the moves he saw the next day.

When Cristiano disappeared around a bend in the road up the hill, Jose Dinis gave chase. He finally caught up with him as he turned onto Lombinho Street where the older neighbourhood kids were playing a pick-up game. He hung back so his son wouldn't see him.

The older boys had set up bins to mark the goal boundaries. They were getting ready to start. Instead of watching, Cristiano dropped his ball and kicked it over all the kids' heads. The ball ricocheted off one bin, forcefully knocking it over, then proceeded to trickle into the makeshift goal. Cristiano raised both arms into the air and ran around the street with pure joy.

The older boys gawked and laughed. So did Jose Dinis from his vantage point. Cristiano ran straight to the goal and retrieved his ball. Then he walked past them. And when he got to Adelino, the boy who had laughed at him, he smiled at him victoriously. Then he marched back down the hill towards his house. Jose Dinis pulled alongside him and Cristiano grinned up at his father. 'Thanks for the ball, Dad,' he said. Cristiano was already tall for his age and Jose Dinis draped his arm over his son's shoulders and squeezed. 'Nice shot,' he said evenly, pretending to be not impressed.

'Thanks,' Cristiano said, poker-faced.

They walked along in silence for a few moments. But Jose Dinis could no longer hold it in. 'Who am I kidding?' Jose Dinis said. 'It was a great shot!' He squeezed his son tighter.

CHAPTER 4

In the spring that Cristiano Ronaldo turned six, he stretched out on his bed and juggled the ball with his feet. He heard his mother and father arguing in the kitchen. His father had been drinking again. It was near dinnertime and his mum was preparing the meal. They always fought about money. His mum begged his dad to stop drinking. Most of the money he earned as a gardener and kit man, he spent on alcohol. His mum's salary went towards buying food and paying the bills – but it was never enough. She worked from dawn until dusk, cooking and cleaning homes. She worked hard and did everything in her power to give her family everything she could. But his father couldn't help it.

His father promised to stop drinking, but he

could never keep his promise. It was sad. He looked horrible when he drank and Cristiano hated it. When he looked at his father, he knew he wasn't himself. He loved his father and hoped he would stop his habit. Even at his young age, he knew it was bad for his father's health. He saw the despair in his father's eyes and felt desperate and confused because he couldn't help him.

He swore to himself that he would never drink anything alcoholic. Not a glass. Not a drop. Ever.

He hated being poor. He knew there was a way out. Although they never went hungry, he knew there were people who always had more than enough food on the table and never worried about empty stomachs. They ate everything they liked, when they liked. They slept in nice beds in big houses where the rain stayed outside. There had to be a way out. But how? Seeing his parents and his brother and sisters suffer gave him great pain. He vowed that one day he would grow up and change all that. They would all live in beautiful homes. His mum and dad would be happy and stop arguing.

His dad would get over his drinking problems and finally be a happy, sober, and healthy man.

He had to get out. He ran to the window and looked out at the street in front of his house as the usual group of older boys moved up Rua Quinta Falcão to Lombinho. He charged back through the room to his bedroom, grabbed his ball, and scurried across the room back to the window.

He smelled the strong aromas of fennel and kale streaming from the kitchen into his bedroom and he knew it would only be a matter of time before his mother called him. He didn't want to eat. He wanted to play. Playing always made him happy. It was his way to escape – a way to forget the desperation and the shadows. The street was bright and welcoming. The kids were tough, but he was tough too. Playing in the street was sheer happiness – an island of joy. He could play there for hours and forget how hard life was back at home.

'Elma! Katia! Come set the table! Hugo! Cristiano! Come help me! Dinner is almost ready!' his mum shouted as she stirred the pot.

Cristiano was already halfway out the window

by the time his mother had called his name, and all the way into the street, before she knew he was no longer in the house.

'Mama, Cristiano went out the window with his ball again,' Katia tattled.

'I'll get him,' Hugo said, charging for the door.

'Hugo, wait!' Dolores said.

Hugo stopped in his tracks and obediently turned around, confused. 'Why?'

'Let him go. Playing ball makes him happy. I'll get him after we eat,' she said, passing a pile of bowls to her daughters.

The street had been in disrepair for as long as Cristiano could remember: potholes littered the road, the walls tagged by various Santo Antonio street gangs. Cristiano had a favourite wall where he practised his kicks. It was just up the street from his house. He began his daily routine of kicking the ball against the stone wall with his right foot, catching it with his left, rolling it over back to his right, lifting it up skillfully, and letting it land on his head.

He paid no attention to the boys who were

coming up the hill on their way to their own pick-up game. Cristiano saw them out of the corner of his eye and retrieved his ball. 'Hey! Guess what? I'm six! Wait up!' He ran up the hill, quickly touching the ball back and forth between his left foot and his right foot. When he pulled alongside the older boys, he balanced the ball smoothly on the laces of his right shoe, kicked it over to his left, and immediately launched it into the air where he caught it on his head. 'I'm old enough now!' he said.

'What are you talking about, Cristiano?' asked Adelino.

Cristiano grinned. 'You said I could play with you when I was six. Well, I'm six.'

The boys all laughed.

Adelino shushed the boys. 'Those were some serious moves,' he said, taking the ball from Cristiano. 'You've been practising.'

'Every day. If I miss, it goes down the hill and I don't get it back,' he said. 'So far, no misses.' He felt like he was in heaven. The obvious leader of the group had just said he was good enough.

'But we're nine now,' Adelino said and tossed the ball back to him. 'Come back when you're nine.'

The boys laughed and continued up the street.

Cristiano felt his face turn red and he boiled inside. Even though he was only six years old, he knew he would never catch up with them in age. He had to go against them now. He dropped the ball without taking his eyes off the older boys. Instinctively, he kicked the ball and it sailed up the hill and hit Adelino in the back.

All the boys stopped and looked at each other, waiting to see what Adelino would do.

Adelino turned around slowly.

Cristiano stood his ground. 'When I'm nine, you'll be twelve and you'll say the same thing!' he shouted.

Adelino narrowed his eyes as if he was going to explode in anger. Instead, he laughed. He laughed so hard he fell over. The other boys laughed too. Adelino took Cristiano's beat-up old ball and bowled it down the incline back to the six-year-old. Cristiano stopped the rolling ball expertly with his instep.

'Okay, Cristiano!' he shouted. 'You're six! So help us win!' With that, he turned and continued walking towards Lombinho Street.

Cristiano stood frozen in the middle of the street holding his ball close to his chest. He had known Adelino his whole life. Their families lived on the same street. He knew him as the guy who walked by his house every day on his way to the next game. He thought he was dreaming. Was he just invited to play?

Up the hill, Adelino turned his head slightly as he walked. 'You coming or not?'

Cristiano sucked in a deep breath, wiped away the tears that always came when he got worked-up, and raced up the hill. He caught up with the older neighbourhood boys just before they turned onto the next street. Adelino grinned and draped his arm over Cristiano's shoulders. 'Nice shot,' he said. They shared a laugh, then marched around the corner and disappeared up Lombinho Street.

The other guys were waiting for them. They stood near some old bricks that marked a goal. A couple of the guys were passing the ball back and forth between them. When Adelino's team arrived, they all stopped. Every guy on the other team was at least twelve years old. Cristiano's heart raced... twelve-year-olds scared him.

'Hey, no babies allowed!' said one of the boys, pointing at Cristiano.

Cristiano clenched his fists. He wanted to throw something. But then he would probably get beaten up and he didn't want that. So he kept his mouth shut.

'Cristiano is no baby, Vagabundo!' Adelino shouted back. 'You better watch your back!' Then he turned to Cristiano. 'Stay in the middle and if the ball comes to you, find one of us.'

'I know how to play,' Cristiano said, marching himself into position.

Seconds later, the other team's goalie punted the ball into the air and it bounced off Adelino and landed at the other boy's feet. Cristiano raced over, stole it away from him and expertly manoeuvred the ball to Adelino, who dribbled and shot it at the goal, barely missing the left post.

'Oh man!' Cristiano said, shaking his head.

Adelino hurried past him. 'What are you worried about? We'll get another chance.' That's when he saw Cristiano's face: bitter and angry, streaked with tears.

'Why did you miss? It was a perfect pass!'

'I missed, okay? It's just a game,' he said. 'Calm down!'

'I am calm!'

'Tell that to your face,' Adelino spat back, irritated. 'Like you could do better?' He muttered under his breath.

'Put me up front and watch.'

The two boys stared each other down. All the other boys just stood by and looked on, smiling.

'Up front? You think you can handle it?'

'Better than you,' Cristiano answered back. He meant it.

Adelino locked eyes with him. 'Okay. Switch places with me, mister striker,' he said.

On the way home, Cristiano looked over at Adelino and grinned. Adelino just shook his head. 'Six years old,' he said. 'I hate to think what you're gonna be like when you're nine!' They stopped in front of Cristiano's shanty. Cristiano winked: 'I want to play for Real Madrid.'

'Who doesn't?' Adelino said. The two boys laughed and Adelino slapped Cristiano on the back and ruffled his hair. Cristiano marched up to his front door where his mother was standing on the step waiting for him.

'Why are you so late?'

'I was just kicking around, Mum,' he said.

'You were playing with Adelino and those older boys?' she asked, eyeballing the gang of ruffians as they scattered in various directions back home. She draped her arm over her youngest son's shoulders and squeezed him tight to her side. He was already tall for his age; he was going to need new shoes soon.

'Everyone is older than me, Mum,' he said, pulling her down to his face and kissing her cheek. 'We won,' he said. 'I scored two goals.' He sounded disappointed.

'That's great!' she said.

Cristiano shrugged, disappointed. 'I wanted a hat trick,' he said.

CHAPTER 5

Cristiano's heart raced as he looked down on the Christmas lights of the harbour from his favourite place high atop Rua Quinta Falcão. His sister Elma pulled up next to him, curious as to what he was looking at.

Funchal Harbor was lit up with bright lights all along the shoreline from the resort hotels on the coast in the winter of 1991. A gigantic tree ornament, made entirely of multi-coloured lights, rested slightly askew on the boardwalk that ran along the seaside resort, turning everything orange and red. 'Where have you been?' Elma asked.

'Where else? Playing,' he said, then pointed at the harbour below. 'Look.'

'I have eyes,' she said, giving her younger brother a look, then turned her head and stared at the harbour. 'They are beautiful,' she said. 'Katia, Hugo, and I do this every year. You're usually in bed!'

Cristiano sniffed the air. 'I think I smell fish frying,' he said.

Katia bit her lip. 'You can bet no one is hungry down in the marina tonight,' she said.

Down there were the great kitchens of the fancy hotels where tourists ate their meals, slept on lounges in the sub-tropical sun, and cooked their skin to perfection. They spent more money on a manicure than his parents spent on food in a month. Up on the hill, especially among the shanties in the neighbourhood, it was a daily struggle just to put food on the table. What would it be like to eat down there?

It was not long before all four children were staring down the hill at the Christmas lights that decorated the Funchal marina. Cristiano shifted his gaze and stared at a Christmas tree in the big front window of a large yellow house down the street, all covered in colourful lights that mirrored off the silvery strands of tinsel. He wished they had a tree. But he knew they wouldn't be getting one.

'Is Father Christmas coming tonight?' Cristiano asked.

Elma looked to Katia and to Hugo. She knew there would be no presents tonight. There were never any presents. Their father could not afford a tree, let alone presents. She wrapped her arms around him. 'I don't know, Cristiano, but I do know this – it won't always be this way.'

Somewhere on the mountain above them, lightning flashed across the sky, then came the usual loud peals of thunder.

'Let's go,' Elma said, taking Cristiano's hand and nudging her sister and brother with her knee. 'Let's go in. It is going to rain.'

'What's the difference?' Hugo said, getting up from his vantage point. 'It rains just as much on the inside as it does on the outside.'

Cristiano twisted out of Elma's lap. 'I'll get the pots out!' he shouted and raced into the house, dodging raindrops.

Elma, Hugo, and Katia laughed and followed him

in. They could always count on him to be cheerful. Later that night, the cooking pots and pans that were placed strategically around the floor under the leaks, played a concerto as the rain poured in.

Much later, after the rain had stopped and the moon came out and turned everything blue outside, Dolores got up to get a drink of water and decided to look in on the children, padding quietly into their room. They were all asleep. She went over to Cristiano who had his football wrapped in his arms, sleeping soundly with a smile on his face. She bent down and kissed his forehead.

He thrashed and kicked out and caused Elma to stir, who caused Katia to stir, who caused Hugo to yell something in his sleep. She watched the foursome settle down and sleep peacefully again. She wanted something better for them than this – all crowded into one room in the same bed, but it just did not seem possible, not on what she and Dinis made cleaning homes and keeping grounds at Andorinha.

In the morning, Fernão showed up bright and early and knocked three times on the Aveiro front door. He had something hidden behind his back. He knew who would answer the door – the first one up – always.

Cristiano raced from his bed to the front door and threw it open and there was his godfather.

'You didn't even ask who it was before you opened the door,' Fernão scolded. 'What if I had been a burglar?'

'You couldn't have been – there's nothing here to steal!'

Fernão laughed and stepped into the home, his hands still hidden behind his back. He scanned the room. 'Where is the tree?'

'Who needs a tree?' Cristiano said.

'No one *needs* a tree,' Fernão said, chuckling. 'Where are the presents?'

'Who needs presents?' Cristiano said, trying to see what Fernão had behind his back.

'Nobody *needs* presents,' he said, whipping his hands in front of him. He was holding a wrapped present. 'You *want* presents.'

Cristiano eyeballed the present. 'Who is that for?'

'Who do you think?' Fernão said, pushing it at him.

Cristiano grabbed the box and tore the wrapping paper off. There was a clear window in the top of the box and inside – a bright red remote-controlled race car.

'A car,' Cristiano said.

Fernão detected a hint of disappointment.

Cristiano set the present down on the table. 'Now we have a present!'

'Aren't you going to open it and play with it?'

Cristiano shook his head. 'Wait here.' He raced off into his room.

'Where am I going to go?' Fernão said to himself.

Cristiano hurried back into the room with his football. 'This is *my* present,' he said. 'Give the car to Hugo. He likes cars.'

Fernão studied his godson for a moment, and then nodded. 'What was I thinking?' he said.

'Yeah,' Cristiano said, laughing. 'What *were* you thinking? You know I only like football! That's why I want to play for Real Madrid!'

Fernão laughed and hugged him. 'Who doesn't?!'

Jose Dinis and Dolores came into the room. 'What's all this noise?'

'I found some presents on the front porch. How is Father Christmas supposed to leave them if you lock the door?' he asked, pulling three more small wrapped presents from his coat pockets.

Elma, Katia, and Hugo came in, still half-asleep, and Fernão handed each of them one of the small presents. *'Feliz Natal,'* he said, which was Portuguese for Merry Christmas. He winked at Cristiano and Cristiano winked back.

'Merry Christmas, everyone!' Cristiano said.

CHAPTER 6

Maria Dos Santos, Cristiano's teacher, picked up a
piece of chalk from the tray beneath the blackboard
and studied her class. Cristiano Ronaldo's seat was
empty again. She turned back to the blackboard
and began to scrawl some words on it. There was a
noise and some giggling and she spun around. Out
of nowhere, Cristiano was in his seat, his hands
clasped in front of him, his eyes staring straight at
her, his hair wet, but neatly
combed. 'So nice of you to finally join us, Mr Aveiro.'

'Thank you, Señora Dos Santos,' Cristiano said,
and there were some scattered giggles from around
the class. Then he winked at her.

His wink caught her off-guard. It was so
unexpected! She turned back to the blackboard,
started to write, then spun back around to face the

class. Cristiano was exactly as she had left him. This time, he flashed a smile. She pursed her lips and slowly turned back and resumed her scrawling. If it had been anyone else who was late, she would have sent him to the Principal's office. But she knew of Cristiano's home life, the impossibly small living quarters, the father's drinking; she felt fortunate he showed up at all, considering all he ever thought about was football.

At lunch time, his other classmates sat in a circle on the lawn, eating from sacks and cloth bags. He didn't have a sack lunch but he had trained himself to ignore lunch so he could play instead. There were no balls, so he used his socks. He bounced the sock ball from one foot to the other, again and again and again, perfecting the move while everybody else munched sandwiches and fruit.

'Don't you ever think of anything else, Cristiano?' Glenda, one of his classmates asked, offering to share her apple with him.

'No,' Cristiano said and continued to bounce the sock ball.

After he returned home from school, Cristiano closed the bathroom door behind him and looked down at the ball at his feet. There was barely enough room for a person, let alone a person and a ball in there. He wanted to perfect the Cruyff move, then make it better. The move, named after its architect, Johan Cruyff, the legendary Dutch attacking midfielder, was designed to give the opposing team a migraine. To do this, he needed a small space. Cristiano raised one leg as if he was going to fake a pass, then tapped the ball behind the other leg in a quick change of direction. Then he alternated feet, first using his right foot to move left, then his left foot to move right. He did it hundreds of times in the tiny bathroom.

Dolores was in the kitchen chopping vegetables. What was that noise coming from in the bathroom? She put her knife down and hurried over to the closed bathroom door. 'What are you *doing* in there?' she shouted through the door.

'Practising,' Cristiano shouted back.

Out in the street, Adelino and the boys stopped in front of the Aveiro house. 'Cristiannnnooo!!'

Adelino yelled.

Cristiano threw open the bathroom door, grabbed his ball and darted out, flashing a smile at his mum as he hurried past her and out the front door.

Out in the street, the boys had already started a game. 'It's too muddy up on Lombinho!' Adelino shouted.

A taxi cab horn blared and Cristiano and Adelino scrambled out of the way. After the cars passed, the game resumed and two defenders from the other team ganged up on Cristiano as soon as he got the ball. He had to figure out how to trick them. The goal was uphill from him so he dribbled the ball up the steep incline. There was an old car tyre on the side of the road so Cristiano instinctively played the ball off the tyre, controlling it again on the other side of the astonished defenders.

Adelino stopped in his tracks. 'How did you think of something like that?'

'I didn't have a choice,' Cristiano said.

As three other defenders charged at him, he used his newly perfected move to evade them. Closely controlling the ball, manoeuvring right, Cristiano raised his right foot, dummying a pass, and then skillfully touched the ball behind his other leg, changing direction instantly. He took two more quick dribbles, and, looking over his shoulder, lightly tapped the ball between the cans. All the other defenders were behind him, trying to catch up.

Adelino grabbed him and shook him like a bottle of soda pop. 'That was *amazing!'* he said as they marched back down to the midline, his arm draped over his pal's shoulders. 'You just blew my mind!' he said. 'You did it so fast, I almost didn't see it!'

Cristiano shrugged. All that bathroom practice paid off.

Adelino stopped and took his friend by the shoulders again and got close so no one else could hear. 'Don't do it too much,' he warned. 'Bring it out when we really need it – and the others won't know what hit them!'

The game resumed. It was only a matter of seconds before Cristiano got the ball again and started dribbling. The opposing team formed a human wall in front of him and he needed to find a quick way around them. He was ready with the step-over. In a flash, he circled over the ball with his left foot and without stopping, did the same with his right foot, finishing off the manoeuvre by tapping the ball with his left, evading the wall. Instantaneously, he was alone in front of the goal and tapped it in for another easy score.

Cristiano's cousin, Nuno, could not believe his eyes. He saw the whole thing from across the street. His little cousin was doing things with his feet he had never seen before. That was when Cristiano's father, Jose Dinis, came out.

'Let's go,' he said to Nuno. 'You've got a game to play.'

'Sure,' Nuno said, never taking his eyes off Cristiano out in the street. The game had resumed and Cristiano had stolen the ball again. He stood there watching Cristiano rocket through the opposition. 'What about Cristiano?'

'What about him?' Jose Dinis asked.

'He can play with us,' Nuno said, matter-of-factly. 'At Andorinha!'

Jose Dinis gave him a look and realized his nephew was serious. 'Let me think about it,' he said. They walked down the street towards the Andorinha pitch. Cristiano watched them go. He had heard it all.

When the weekend came, Nuno didn't wait for his uncle to make a decision. He snuck into Cristiano's room on his hands and knees and made his way across the floor to where his young cousin was sleeping. 'Psst!'

Cristiano did not stir.

'PSSSST!' Nuno said again, this time much louder.

One of Cristiano's eyes fluttered open but stared nowhere.

'That is totally weird,' Nuno said and backed up a little.

Cristiano woke up with a start and began to shout and Nuno clapped his hand over his mouth. 'Shhhh,' he whispered.

'What do you want, Nuno?'

'I got a game in an hour. Want to watch me play?'

Cristiano's eyes widened and he threw off his covers and leapt to his feet. He wore underwear that had pictures of cartoon characters all over them. Nuno swallowed his laugh. 'I'll take that as a yes.'

Cristiano nodded with excitement.

'Meet me outside in a few minutes,' Nuno said. 'And *hurry*. We're already late.'

Cristiano nodded. And then it hit him and he jumped out of bed like a rocket.

CHAPTER 7

Coach Francisco Afonso was on the Andorinha
sideline with Cristiano's godfather, Fernão, and Jose
Dinis. They had split the Andorinha youth team
into two squads of eight-year-olds and were in the
middle of a heated practice game when six-year-old
Cristiano arrived.

Nuno led the charge down the pitch towards the
goal. Cristiano wanted to rush out there so badly,
he felt like he was going to jump out of his skin:
a real pitch with grass instead of a street, a pitch
where he could dodge defenders instead of rubbish
bins cans and old car tyres. When Cristiano saw his
cousin, he could no longer control his excitement
and he leapt to his feet and cheered.

Nuno scored a goal, turned back, saw his cousin
Cristiano in the stands, and waved to him. The kid

was bouncing up and down like a Jack-in-the-box and it made him laugh.

Cristiano's father and Nuno asked him to come over during the practice break. 'You want to practise with Nuno, Cristiano?' his father asked.

Cristiano felt his heart race. These guys were all older than him, but he was used to that now. In fact, he could not remember a time that he played with boys his own age. He clamoured out of the stands before he realized what he was doing. His body was already moving before his brain caught up. 'Yes!' he shouted.

Nuno punched his cousin's shoulder. 'Come on, then.'

'Are you sure it's okay?' Cristiano asked his dad, walking gingerly out on the pitch. The rest of Nuno's team waved him to come over. His godfather, Fernão, watched intently as Cristiano joined Nuno's squad.

The scrimmage resumed.

Cristiano scanned the stands and spotted his mother just arriving and sitting down in the bleachers next to Alvaro Milho, the youth director.

Cristiano was as fast as lightning as he ran down the flank, evading defenders, the ball glued to his feet. When the last defender tried to tackle him, he stood still for an instant, stared down the defender, rolled the ball between his legs, controlled it on the other side, completed the nutmeg, and burst into the box.

One-on-one with the goalkeeper, he struck the ball hard and low to the far post, showing perfect form. The ball flew into the corner of the net. Sweet! he thought. He loved the feeling of beating the keeper!

He shot a quick look over at the stands. His mum and Milho smiled back at him. The rest of the team slammed into him and took him to the ground. Nuno skidded to a stop, reached out a hand, and pulled his little cousin back up to his feet. 'Well played, cousin! Well played!'

The rest of the game went just like that. Cristiano scored two more goals and when he got his hat trick, Milho waved Jose Dinis, Fernão, and Coach Afonso over to him. 'Your boy is amazing!' he blubbered to Jose Dinis. 'We want him!'

CHAPTER 8

Cristiano slept facedown with his bum in the air, his arms outstretched on either side of him like airplane wings, a wadded-up blanket over his head like an ill-fitting turban. A car skidded to a stop outside. Cristiano stirred. The front door swung open and he heard dreamlike footsteps and thought a giant was going to step on his house and crush it.

Milho stepped into the room and found his seven-year-old football player asleep on the floor in an impossible position. 'ROLL IT OUT!' he shouted and Cristiano flew off the floor like a cat that had just been shocked by a jolt of static electricity.

Milho snatched a half-filled plastic water bottle from a nearby chair and poured it over the kid's head.

Cristiano sputtered awake, shocked, and sat bolt

upright. 'Help! I'm drowning!' Then he blinked away the water and Milho came into focus. He quickly tried to dive back under the covers, but Milho grabbed him by the scruff of his shirt. 'Oh no, you don't!' he said, yanking the boy to his feet.

'Let me go! Let me go!' Cristiano said, struggling.

'You are late for the game! Everyone is waiting for you!'

Cristiano streaked like an arrow to the bathroom. 'I'll be ready in a minute, coach!'

Milho smiled.

Cristiano attacked along the sideline. The other team could not keep up. He loved the feeling of the air against his face as he ran along the touchline.

His coach, Francisco Afonso, watched him from the sidelines. Cristiano's head bobbed up and down as he towered over the other boys his age. He was incredibly fast for a seven-year-old. They had nicknamed him the *Little Bee* because no one could catch him.

The players from Camacha FC arrived by bus from their little village in the hills, a few miles east of Funchal. Afonso scanned the stands and saw Milho sitting next to Cristiano's mother. Then he saw who was sitting on the other side of her: the President of Andorinha himself, Rui Santos. He was surprised. Rui Santos hardly ever came to watch the youth team play. The team had been losing lately, despite Cristiano playing every game. A little swallow had told him that Cristiano was not happy and was talking about leaving the team. Rui Santos was there to keep his star.

Afonso scanned the pitch and saw Cristiano's father near the equipment room, straightening up. Cristiano went around the side of the stands but instead of going out, he stayed in the shadows and watched. Jose Dinis spotted him from the equipment shed and hurried over. 'What's up, Cristiano? You should be out there,' he said.

'I don't want to play, Dad,' Cristiano blurted out.

'Don't be silly, they need you,' Jose Dinis said, taking his son by the shoulders. Then he saw the look in his son's eyes and knew the situation was serious. 'You know, I've never heard you pass up a game. Not one. Not even when you were sick.'

Cristiano took a long time to answer. 'But we always lose,' he said and tears streaked down his cheeks. 'I don't want to lose anymore.'

Jose Dinis studied his son and gathered his thoughts. 'But they can't get better without you. What do I always say about the weak?'

'Only the weak quit?'

'That's right. You can't quit now.'

Cristiano knew his father was right. He got angry thinking about all the mistakes his teammates made on the pitch. But leaving the team wouldn't fix anything because it wasn't their fault. This wasn't like the streets of Madeira where if you made a mistake, you got beaten up. He had to help them. 'You're right,' he said to his father, then trotted over to the wing, his place on the pitch. He got the ball in the first five seconds of play. The Camacho boys did not know what hit them as he blew through them, dribbling the ball majestically between his feet. He passed the ball to the striker, who was free right in front of the goal, but he shot the ball high above the post. Sure enough, the Camacho counter-attack ended with a goal.

Cristiano held in his anger and tried to hold back tears. A miss like this was the worst thing he could think of in the world right then. He couldn't hold them back.

In the stands, Dolores and Rui Santos were on their feet. They watched Cristiano intently. 'What is he doing out there?' Rui Santos asked.

'Crying,' Dolores said.

'Crying?' Rui Santos asked.

Dolores nodded, slightly embarrassed.

It was halftime and Andorinha was down two-nil, despite Cristiano's best efforts.

Rui Santos got up, left his seat, and headed straight for Cristiano who was just coming off the pitch. 'Cristiano,' he said.

'Yes sir,' Cristiano said, wiping his face with his sleeve.

'Why are you crying?'

Cristiano riveted the club president with a look

that startled him. 'I am angry because we are losing, sir,' the boy said.

'But it's only half time, and what? You are down two? There's plenty of time to win this thing.' Then Rui Santos thought he realized what Cristiano was saying. 'Wait a minute,' he said. 'It's your teammates, isn't it? Look, you know, there aren't any other boys here who play as well as you.'

'I know, that's why I'm angry,' Cristiano said.

'At your teammates?'

'No. At myself. For being angry at them.'

Rui Santos smiled at Cristiano. 'I think I know what you mean.'

Cristiano studied him for a moment and nodded. He wiped his tears and excused himself, then jogged over to his teammates who were getting ready for the second half. As soon as the referee's whistle announced the start of the second half, Cristiano, in an incredible solo dribbling effort, marched like a general through enemy territory and single handedly managed to evade every opponent. He finished the awe-inspiring move with a strike to the top right corner.

Rui Santos was on his feet, amazed.

The team surrounded him and when he emerged from the pack, he flashed a smile at his mum in the stands and raised one finger in the air. He scored two more times and Andorinha won.

CHAPTER 9

Cristiano's godfather, Fernão, came for a visit.
He had left Andorinha for a scouting job with
Nacional the previous year. Now he was a man
on a mission.

'We miss you, Fernão,' Jose Dinis said as the
two old friends hugged. 'How is Nacional treating
you?'

Dolores, Jose Dinis, and Fernão sat in the main
room. Fernão could feel the tension in the little
room. 'Nacional is OK,' he said, 'But you know
why I came.'

'Yes, we do,' Jose Dinis said. 'And you know
how much I love *you,* Fernão, but the answer is no.
If Cristiano has to go to a bigger team it has to be
my team, Maritimo.'

'Never,' Dolores said. Nacional was her team.

The Maritimo green and red were out of the question for her.

'Maritimo's scout was at Andorinha yesterday,' Jose Dinis said. 'He met with the president.'

Fernão sighed. 'Let's talk to Cristiano. I want to know what he thinks.'

Minutes later Cristiano showed up with his ball. He was happy to see his godfather.

'Are you taking me to Nacional?' he asked eagerly.

'Maybe,' Fernão said. 'But Maritimo wants you too. Your mother and father will never be able to decide for you, because each of them loves their own home team too much. It's going to have to be up to you.'

Jose Dinis and Dolores knew Fernão was right and both of them turned to their youngest son.

'What do you think, Cristiano?' Fernão asked. 'Which team do *you* want to join?'

'I will go with the team that wants me the most,' Cristiano said.

No one said a word for a moment.

'OK. So now let me speak as your godfather, not as a Nacional scout,' Fernão said and turned to the parents. 'You should ask both teams to meet with you and we will see for ourselves which team wants Cristiano more. How does that sound?'

Dolores and Jose Dinis exchanged looks. Fernão could always be trusted to come up with the right idea.

Cristiano saw his mum smile and then his dad. He nodded his agreement.

'It's a win-win,' said Fernão.

Cristiano smiled. He loved the word *win* and Fernão said it twice.

Cristiano sat with his parents and Rui Santos, the president of Andorinha, at a table in the best restaurant in the Funchal Marina. The smell of the food drove him crazy. They were familiar aromas. He had smelled them all the way up at Rua Quinta Falcão. They smelled much better down here. Everything on the menu looked delicious and he felt great.

'What would you like to eat, Cristiano?' Rui Santos asked.

'Everything,' Cristiano said. 'Start with the *bacalhau*. And this time put some fish in it.'

A few minutes later, Rui Alves, the President of Nacional showed up with Fernão. Alves wanted to sit next to Cristiano.

'Where are the Maritimo people?' Santos asked, looking around the table.

Rui Alves picked up a menu. 'Maritimo cancelled at the last minute,' he said offhandedly. 'I just spoke with them. They decided they had more pressing business.'

'What?!' Jose Dinis said. 'They blew us off?!' he was clearly upset.

'Afraid so,' Fernão said. 'Maritimo went to scout some talent in Brazil instead.' He took a sip of water.

'They don't want me?' Cristiano asked.

Rui Alves could not hide his delight. 'Maybe they don't, Cristiano, but we do.'

Cristiano flashed him a grin. He had never seen his mother happier. Maritimo had not shown up, but the team that wanted him the most had – Nacional.

Rui Alves smiled broadly. In the morning, he would strike a deal to bring Cristiano Ronaldo to Nacional, and Cristiano Ronaldo's life would change forever.

Cristiano had heard from his godfather that Clube Desportivo Nacional thought he was scrawny, so he showed up for his first practice five pounds heavier. He ate everything in sight. Even his vegetables. As soon as he took the field for a practice game, he scored the first goal in the first fifteen seconds. When he ran back to get ready for the next play, Coach Talhinhas was waiting for him: 'I like the way you play, but you need to learn how to pass the ball,' he said. 'You don't have to do everything alone.'

In the first three matches with Cristiano playing midfield, Nacional won every match easily. He was their top goal-scorer, but he was also a ball hog. His teammates did not love the fact that the new talent did everything alone, although they did love winning. And when they lost, oh boy. Their new teammate always cried. He could not stand to lose and he could not control his tears. It earned him the nickname, *Cry Baby.*

Cristiano's second and last season with the team, at age nine, was their best season ever and he led Nacional to win the Youth League title.

Jose Dinis and Dolores walked back to the parking lot from the awards ceremony with their son between them. Fernão was waiting for them.

Dolores kissed Cristiano on the forehead and Jose Dinis hugged him tighter than he had ever hugged him before. 'Go with Fernão. We will see you at home,' his father said. Then he took Dolores' hand and walked to their car. Cristiano watched them go, then turned back to Fernão.

'Congratulations on the win, Cristiano,' Fernão said, opening the passenger door for him. Cristiano climbed in and Fernão started the engine.

'Let's talk,' he said.

'Okay,' he said warily.

'I know why you don't pass the ball,' Fernão said without hesitation.

'We talked it over!' Cristiano blurted out. 'Me and the team – we do what it takes to win!'

'I know they want to win just as much as you do,' Fernão said. 'But what is acceptable for the

Nacional youth team isn't good enough for bigger and better teams. Let me ask you something: you don't plan on playing for Nacional your whole life, do you?'

'No! I want to play for Real Madrid!' Cristiano exclaimed.

Fernão laughed. 'Who doesn't? But you don't get to Real Madrid from here.'

'Who says?' Cristiano said with a twinkle in his eye.

Fernão laughed again. 'Hold on to that thought!' He pulled the car out of the lot and started the short drive up the hill to Rua Quinta Falcão.

After they drove in silence for a few minutes, Fernão opened up: 'I have a question for you.'

Cristiano turned from the window. 'Okay,' he said.

'Do you want to be great?'

'More than anything,' Cristiano answered.

'Do you know what greatness is?'

'Playing great.'

'Yes, some of it is playing great. But football is a team sport,' Fernão replied. 'If you don't get that – then you don't get the game. If you want to be great, you have to help your teammates *play* great.'

He pulled the car up to the front of Cristiano's home and stopped.

Cristiano's eyes welled-up with tears. 'I don't win just for me. I win for the whole team!'

'I know you do, Cristiano. Just think ahead,' Fernão said.

'I will,' Cristiano promised. He was dead serious and his godfather knew the boy was eager to learn.

There was enormous talent burning inside him, Fernão thought. Willpower too. With the right environment – and the right team – this talent could translate into self-discipline and a great work ethic.

After he dropped Cristiano off, Fernão drove straight home and made the phone call he had been hoping to make. He called his old friend, Joao Marques de Freitas, a local magistrate and the president of the Sporting Lisbon club in Funchal. Fernão had only two words to say to him and de Freitas knew exactly what he meant:

'He's ready.'

CHAPTER 10

Cristiano saw him first but he did not know who he was. Later, his sister Elma told him everything about the day the man from Sporting Lisbon came to call.

Paolo Cardoso arrived on Madeira without warning. He wanted to see the kid from Rua Quinta Falcão. He wanted to see him play without any interference from his family or his godfather, Fernão de Sousa, whom he knew quite well. He sat in the stands and took notes on the boy who played in the central midfield as if he was born there. As soon as the game ended, Cardoso walked down the rows of the stands to where Fernão, Jose Dinis, Dolores, Elma, and the kids sat.

Fernão recognized him immediately, stood up,

and shook his hand. 'Paolo, I did not know you were on the island!'

Cardoso sat down next to Fernão. 'You weren't supposed to know,' he said softly.

'I guess I don't have to ask you what you think,' Fernão said.

Cardoso looked from Fernão to Jose Dinis to Dolores and to the kids. 'I think we would like to invite this incredible boy to a tryout.'

'A tryout?' Jose Dinis said. 'Where?'

'Lisbon. For four days. That's all we need.'

'Oh my God,' Dolores said. 'Sporting Lisbon? Am I dreaming?' She grabbed her husband's hand tightly.

Cardoso smiled politely. 'We will have some fun.'

That night, the Aveiro family and Fernão joined the man from Sporting Lisbon for dinner in the marina. Cristiano brought his ball. The restaurant was in the finest hotel in Funchal and Cristiano ordered swordfish.

'He is only eleven,' Jose Dinis said. 'He has never left the island. And I cannot get away.'

Dolores patted his hand. 'Nobody expects you to,

Dinis. I will go for you. Sporting is not your team anyway.'

Everyone laughed.

'If he stays in Madeira,' said Fernão. 'He will never get the training he needs to become a professional player.'

Cristiano remembered the night well, some years later. He wanted to play for Sporting and he had no idea how bad his life would get. But in that restaurant, at that moment, all he could see were his dreams rushing towards him.

'Remember, this is a tryout,' Cardoso said. 'There are no guarantees.'

'I'm not worried,' Cristiano said. 'I'll make the team.'

No one said a word for a moment.

'I like your confidence,' Cardoso said. 'I'll bet you have a lot of friends. Who's your best friend?'

Cristiano didn't even have to think. He reached down and grabbed the ball he had between his feet and showed it to him. '*This* is my best friend,' he said.

Everyone at the table chuckled.

'Oh, I almost forgot. You're going too,' Cardoso said to Fernão. 'And Dolores. Once he's settled at the academy, you can return home.'

Fernão thought about it and shrugged. 'I'm not going to complain. I could use a holiday.'

A few days later, Cristiano gripped the arm rests of his seat so tightly his fingers turned white. The jet engines fired up and the aircraft taxied down the Funchal runway. He looked out the window and watched the ground whoosh away in a matter of seconds and a few seconds after that, the volcano drifted past below him. It looked fake and far away. Then the plane veered east and circled back over the island before heading for mainland Portugal. Cristiano had never seen his birthplace this way: an island, surrounded by dark blue Atlantic water.

'Did you get any sleep last night?'

'No, Mum,' he answered and leaned against her and closed his eyes. Fernão sat in the aisle seat and read a football magazine.

The flight lasted an hour and forty minutes and they took the bus to the Campo Grande Station adjacent to the Alvalade Stadium at the Sporting Lisbon youth training camp. When the threesome emerged out of the Alvalade station, they saw the grand old *Estádio José Alvalade* stadium in one direction and the training grounds in the other. The temperature was perfect – 75 degrees with a light breeze. Easter decorations were everywhere as the holidays approached. It was 1996.

Dolores had her arm around her son. He had never been off the island and she could tell he was nervous. She watched him and tried to see his new home through his eyes. Her little boy was vanishing right before her eyes. 'You are growing up so fast,' she cooed to him.

'I'm eleven. It means I have responsibilities,' he said proudly.

The grand old stadium rose up in the distance, surrounded by the Sporting Lisbon training grounds. Everything was so big. At Andorinha, Cristiano rose up over all the other players because he was tall for his age, but here, he felt dwarfed by the history and it felt like a dream.

A little while later, Cristiano came out on the

training pitch and there was Paolo Cardoso and another coach, Osvaldo Silva, standing on the sideline. He knew they would have their eyes glued to him. He looked around some more and found his mother sitting in a chair a little way away and that calmed his nerves down. It seemed every time he moved up a rung on the ladder, there were a bunch of adults watching his every move and it made him nervous.

He stood with some of the other players before the tryout began and Silva squinted to see him. 'There's not much to him,' he said. Even though Cristiano had put on weight at Nacional, he grew so tall so fast, it did not seem to matter.

'Wait till you see him play,' Fernão chimed in.

Cardoso grinned at his friend and slapped his back. 'I knew there was a reason why I wanted you here.'

As soon as the ball was in play, Cristiano, fearless, charged in and got hold of it. He made his move down the pitch, driving the ball forward. Whenever anyone got close, he feinted left or right and again found himself in open space. Everyone looked helpless when he scored his first goal.

Osvaldo Silva almost tripped over himself the first time he saw him.

'Okay, that got my attention,' Silva said.

'He's different,' Cardoso said, nodding, getting more and more excited the more he watched Cristiano on the pitch. 'Look how he uses both feet! I want to see him again. Tomorrow. On the other pitch.'

The boys walked in from the pitch. Cristiano was in the middle of all of them, like a conquering hero. 'You are amazing!' one boy said.

'Thanks,' Cristiano said.

'Yeah, but you talk funny.'

Cristiano stopped. 'No, I don't. You do. I'm from the islands,' he said proudly. 'Madeira.'

Sporting had never paid for a youth player, *ever,* but this time around, they paid the young prodigy Cristiano Ronaldo the hefty sum of 27,000 Euros, which they settled against a debt Nacional owed them. This was great news for Cristiano, who impressed everyone at Sporting during the tryout.

Back home, Cristiano and his family were elated when they got the news that they had reached a deal. He never suspected the joyous moment would soon turn into fear and sadness.

His father broke the news to him. For the first time in his life, Cristiano was going to live far away from his family. His parents could not afford to move the whole family to Lisbon.

CHAPTER 11

In August 1997, Cristiano arrived at the Sporting Lisbon youth training grounds alone. He was terrified.

He went straight to the dorms near the Jose Alvalade Stadium where he would be living. Cristiano peered warily into his room: two bunk beds, two double-sided desks, and two closets. He saw three boys.

On one bunk was Fabio Ferreira. Above Fabio on the top bunk was Jose Semedo. In the next bed was Miguel Paixão. Above him – nobody. It was the only bunk left. It was his. Well, he thought – at least they won't all be in *one* bed. He knew his roommates from the tryout. They were good players. He set his duffel bag down.

The sound of a jet taking off grabbed his attention.

'Airport,' Fabio explained. 'Not far from here.'

'What's your name?' Fabio asked.

'Cristiano Ronaldo.'

Fabio thought for a moment. 'I think Ronnie is better.'

'Yea,' said Jose. 'Ronnie is cool.'

Cristiano shrugged. It was better than Cry Baby.

The first thing that came to Cristiano's mind was *escape*. When he kissed his mother and father goodbye at the Funchal airport, they wept. And every time they wept, he wept. He absently checked the time. Was it too soon to call his mother? If he wanted to escape, how would he do it? He nervously turned a plastic card over and over in his hand, working out various scenarios of escaping from the grounds, walking to the airport, and making a call to Madeira, begging someone to buy him a ticket home.

'What's that?' Miguel asked.

'Phone card,' Cristiano said.

'Not much time to make phone calls around here,' said Jose.

'Why?'

'Practice in the morning, school from 10am to 5pm, then more practice. Every day.'

'School,' Cristiano said with a chill in his voice. Fernão had told him about the school at Sporting. It was as important as playing.

'You'll like the school here,' Fabio said. 'Everyone is really nice.'

Two days later, Cristiano stood in front of his class.

'You talk funny,' someone shouted from the back of the class and everyone laughed.

Everyone except Fabio, Jose, and Miguel. And Cristiano.

'I talk funny?' Cristiano asked. 'All I said was "Hello." And sorry I am late for class.'

The whole class laughed again.

'Enough,' the teacher said to the students, opening his book.

Cristiano felt the anger welling up inside him. He glared at the kid in the back who made the crack about his accent. Back on Madeira, if you bad-mouthed like that, you got yourself beaten up. He wanted to run down there, yank him out of his desk, and teach him a lesson. He felt his face turn red just thinking about it.

The teacher had just introduced him as their newest student and the whole class already hated him.

'I don't talk funny. I am from Madeira,' he said and the whole class laughed again. 'Why is that funny?' he shouted at them. 'Madeira is funny?'

'Madeira is beautiful,' someone said. 'The way you *say* it is funny!' Then more laughter. It was mean and Cristiano couldn't take it anymore.

He sensed something moving behind him and he thought someone was coming up behind him, so he grabbed a chair and spun around to stop his attacker.

It was his teacher.

The classroom grew pin-drop quiet.

Finally, the teacher spoke: 'Are you going to hit me with that, Cristiano?'

Cristiano was breathing hard. He slowly put the chair down. He didn't know what to do next.

Tears welled-up in his eyes. He took a deep breath and rushed out of the classroom.

He ran away so fast the tears streaked back across both cheeks and he didn't stop running until he got to the stadium. He slumped against the wall and cried more than he had ever cried. After a few moments, he heard some boys coming this way. They were all talking and laughing. He rushed over to the dressing room and went inside.

The dressing room was smelly and messy. There were wet towels scattered everywhere. Cristiano sat down on a bench to compose himself. Then, when he was calm enough, he would go back to his dorm room – and plan his escape.

'Hey Ronnie!' someone said. 'Give us a hand here and clean up some of these towels.'

Cristiano looked up as Carlos Diaz, one of his coaches, came into the room. He couldn't believe he was being asked to clean up someone else's mess. He glared at Diaz, 'I play for Sporting Lisbon. I'm not your maid!' he spat.

Diaz stopped what he was doing and locked eyes with him.

'Here at Sporting, we *all* help out. Since none of the boys who made this mess are around, you are going to do it.' Diaz was offended.

Cristiano wished he could stuff the words he had said back into his mouth. 'I'm sorry, sir,' he said. 'They made fun of me at school – they disrespected me – because of the way I talk. I – please just leave me alone.'

Diaz studied the new boy. 'Do I look like one of the students who disrespected you?'

Cristiano raised his eyes and looked into Diaz's eyes, then shook his head slowly.

'You know, if you want respect around here, you have to earn it. For refusing an order from a coach, you sit out the next game. And the next time one of your coaches *politely* asks you for help, you think twice about disrespecting *him*.' He left the locker room, angrily picking up dirty towels along the way, finally disappearing around a corner.

Cristiano put his head in his hands and sobbed so loud he heard his own echo. Then he heard footsteps.

'They said I would find you here,' Coach Cardoso said.

Embarrassed, Cristiano stared at the floor.

Cardoso sat down next to him. 'It was wrong of them to make fun of you in class.'

'I want to go home,' Cristiano said.

Cardoso sighed. 'You know, there's always going to be someone who is going to give you a hard time. The question is how you react to it.'

Cristiano stood up. 'I guess I didn't act right.'

Cardoso stood up as well. 'That's a start. I'll tell you what. I have a job for you.'

'A job?'

'On Sundays I want you to be the new ball boy. With the first team. They pay five Euros for each game.'

Cristiano couldn't believe what he was hearing. He knew he was going to get responsibilities. He just didn't realize it would be this soon.

'Now if you'll excuse me, I need to arrange to bring your mother back to Lisbon.'

'My mother?'

'I hear she is lonely. I think it would be better for her and all of us if she came back and stayed here for a while.'

Cristiano fought tears and gulped, 'Thank you.'

CHAPTER 12

Cristiano and his roommates – Miguel, Jose, and Fabio – *all* became ball boys for the first team games. One day, during an exhibition game, Cristiano grabbed a ball that had crossed the line and threw it back to the Sporting first team midfielder waiting at the line to throw it in. Before the midfielder threw it to his winger, he winked at Cristiano and gave him a thumb's up.

After they won the game, the players trotted off the pitch. Cristiano was at the line with the other ball boys holding out their hands. As the players left the pitch, they slapped their hands. When the last man was off the pitch, the ball boys formed a circle. 'This hand,' Cristiano said, holding up his right hand, 'just touched greatness.'

The boys laughed.

'How much do we have if we put our money together? Here's my five,' Cristiano said, holding out a five-Euro note. The other boys produced some more money. Cristiano collected it and counted the bills.

'We have enough,' Cristiano said. 'Let's go.'

The boys raced to the Campo Grande subway station that was a short jog from the stadium, took the green line two stops, and got off. When they charged up the stairs out of the underground station, there was a glorious neon sign right in front of them, sitting atop a restaurant. Cristiano stopped for a moment of reverence with the rest of the ball boys. The sign read *Pizza* in big red letters and flashed brightly. The boys went inside and minutes later emerged with a slice of pizza in each hand, munching away.

'When is the last train out of here?' one of them asked.

'Who cares?' Cristiano said. 'We're walking home.' He finished his first slice and immediately moved on to the second.

The stadium was a mile away, down the two-lane road that wound through a dark grove of trees. When the boys turned a curve in the road, four hoodlums came out of hiding behind them and stood across the road. One of them threw a rock and hit Miguel in the back. He yelled in pain.

Cristiano and his friends turned and stood stock-still as the gang members advanced towards them. They were all carrying sticks and stones. 'You look just like the kind of guys with money in your pockets,' the gang leader said ominously. 'Hand it over and you won't get hurt.'

'What do we do, Ronnie?' Fabio whispered, terrified.

'Get behind me,' Cristiano whispered, pushing him aside. 'I'll handle them.'

His friends all got behind him.

'You want money?' Cristiano shouted at them. 'Get a job!'

The leader of the gang was infuriated and pointed his finger at him and the gang of bullies charged the boys from Sporting Lisbon, waving their sticks.

'Run!' Cristiano shouted at his friends.

The three boys ran down the road towards the stadium.

Cristiano stood there and balled his fists.

The gang members stopped running when they saw Cristiano wasn't moving.

'What's wrong with you?' the leader shouted at him.

Cristiano stood in the middle of the road, 50 feet from them. Four against one. He had faced worse in the streets of Madeira playing a game. And that was with *friends*. 'Bring it,' he said between gritted teeth, reaching down and picking up a fist-sized rock.

The leader did not make a move. They looked from one to the other deciding in their heads what to do.

'Forget it,' the leader finally said. 'He ain't worth it,' he said to his guys and walked away. They followed him without another word.

Cristiano snorted at the retreating hoodlums. A few bullies weren't going to freak him out. He watched them disappear into the night and after he was sure they weren't coming back, he walked back to the dorms.

The story of Cristiano's bravery that night spread rapidly around the dorms of the youth academy at Sporting Lisbon and no one ever made fun of his island accent again.

CHAPTER 13

Cristiano was late to class again.

'Mr Aveiro, I have pretty much had it with your tardiness,' the teacher said.

'Sir, can we please have this talk in private?'

The teacher riveted him. 'No, Mr Aveiro, we have already had those talks, and you are still consistently late. I will have a private talk all right. But it will not be with you, it will be *about* you. Now take your seat and stop disrupting my class or I will ask you to leave.' He turned back to the blackboard and scribbled another sentence on the history of Portugal.

Cristiano glared at his teacher's back. He had had enough too. He hated school and wanted to quit. He had no time for schoolwork; all he could think about was the final round of competition. Sporting had a chance at winning it all this season. When he got back to his dorm room after school, his mother was standing near the window. She had taken the train in from the city where the team provided lodging for her.

'Hi, Mum,' he said. He didn't sound too excited.

'I want to have a little talk with you,' Dolores said.

'If it's about school, I can explain,' he said.

'What *about* school?' she asked, not expecting the subject.

Cristiano did not know what to do. 'Well, I'm not doing so well. What do *you* want to talk about?'

She studied him for moment, forming her words. 'Hugo,' she said.

'What about him?'

'He's not doing so good,' she said. 'He fell in with a bad crowd and, well, we had to put him in rehab. He needs help, Cristiano.'

Cristiano sighed.

'I didn't want you to hear it from someone else. You know how these things get around,' she said. She wasn't very comfortable talking with her youngest son about this subject but it was important to let him know what was happening with his family. He had been away for a while now. 'This kind of thing should stay in the family.'

Cristiano could see this was difficult for his mother and hugged her. 'I know,' he managed.

'You concentrate on school and your training. I'll take care of the family,' she said.

'Okay, Mum. Is that what you came here to tell me?' He knew there was something else.

She looked him right in the eye. 'No,' she said and took a long time to say the rest. 'I can't take care of the family from Lisbon. I'm going home for a while.'

He tried not to show anything, but the thought terrified him. He also knew it was the right thing to do. 'I'll be okay,' he said, even though he wasn't sure at all. 'Besides, we're going to win the championship. And that means we play Maritomo.'

'Maritomo! So you would play against them on the island?' There was hope in her voice.

'Yes. There's no way we are going to lose. I can't wait. Don't worry about me. I'll be home soon and we can take care of Dad and Hugo together.'

Dolores kissed him on the forehead.

A week later, Cristiano was in class when he heard the team roster was about to be posted for the championship game against Maritomo. Every student in class was buzzing. He could see it all: his family and friends sitting in the stands watching him play in a championship game against the home team! *Please forgive me, Dad, for beating your favourite team, but I had to.* It was a pleasant, happy thought. The kid from Rua Quinta Falcão brings home the gold. It was a dream come true.

All of Cristiano's teammates surrounded the bulletin board where the team roster was posted, pointing at it, reading it, walking away happy or disappointed. When Cristiano came up to them, they made room for him to see. He stretched out his finger and ran it down the list of names, one by one, happy for all his friends as he scanned their names. But when he got to the end of the list, he still hadn't seen his own name. This can't be right, he thought. He looked around at his teammates and they wouldn't make eye contact with him. He ran his finger down the list again. He still did not find his name.

'I'm not there,' he heard himself say.

No one else said a word.

He ran his finger down the list two more times, but his name never miraculously appeared. He definitely wasn't on the list.

Fabio stood next to him. 'It must be a mistake, Ronnie.'

Cristiano looked from one teammate to another. He turned and ran down the hallway. He did not want to let them see him crying. He ran all the way to the training centre office. Aurelio Pereira was standing in the doorway when he got there.

'I'm not on the roster! You must've made a mistake!'

'No mistake,' Pereira said coldly.

'But I'm your best player, how could you leave me out?'

'Well, it wasn't an easy decision. But I warned you about school. You are always late or you don't show up. You are disrespectful to the teacher and you disrupt the class. You were disrespectful to your coach. You don't care about school, so we cut you. No school, no play. I've always said that. You won't be travelling with us to Madeira.'

'But my family – '

'Your family already knows. We called them,' Pereira said. 'I think it is time you took a good look at yourself.' He patted Cristiano on the shoulder and Cristiano angrily pulled away.

'We'll talk when we get back,' he said and walked back into his office and closed the door.

Cristiano backed up, collapsed against the wall behind him, and wept. All his dreams of going home and playing against Maritimo were gone.

CHAPTER 14

'The Muslim conquest of Spain began in what year?' the teacher asked.

Cristiano's hand shot up immediately. A few months ago, he moved his seat from the back of the class to the middle.

'Ron?'

'AD 711,' Cristiano said.

'Correct,' the teacher replied.

'Okay, that will be it for the day,' the teacher announced to the class. 'Today is physical day. I'm going to let you out early because the line to the infirmary is already getting kind of long. Dismissed,' he said and the entire class got up and left the classroom.

The line of boys coming out of the infirmary wound like a snake across the small expanse and on to the nearby training pitch. Cristiano filed into the back of the line, just behind Fabio.

An hour later, Cristiano finally marched into the infirmary. The white-painted room had nothing in it but a cabinet and a doctor's table in the middle. The doctor and a nurse stood behind the table.

'Please sit on the table,' the nurse said, flipping a page on her chart. 'Name?'

'You don't recognize me?' Cristiano joked.

'Very funny,' the nurse countered dryly. 'You get an extra shot for being a star,' she said.

'Wait a minute!' Cristiano protested.

'Name?'

'Cristiano Ronaldo dos Santos Aveiro. Ma'am.'

The nurse smiled as she scribbled his name on a page, slapped a blood pressure cuff on him and pumped it up. She took the reading and wrote it down. Passed it to the doctor, who loaded a syringe. Instead of giving him a shot, the doctor put down the syringe and placed two fingers on Cristiano's wrist and took his pulse. After a few moments, he let go and the nurse handed him the clipboard. He wrote something on it. Then he took an instrument and measured the bone in his arm and wrote something down again. 'Good growth,' he said. It was the first time he had spoken. 'You're going to be tall.'

'I'm already tall,' Cristiano said.

The doctor smiled politely and wrote something down on Cristiano's chart. 'I have one issue,' he said without warning. 'Your resting heart rate is too high. I'm going to order some tests.'

'I'm just excited, that's all,' Cristiano said.

The nurse squirted the syringe to get out the air bubbles. Then she plunged the needle into his arm.

'Ow!' Cristiano said.

'How was that?' the nurse asked. 'Superstar.'

Cristiano flashed a big smile, then hopped down and the nurse handed him a slip of paper.

'Next week, someone will drive you in to the city.'

As promised, a week later, Cristiano bounced around in the back of Pereira's car, with Leonel Pontes, his tutor on one side, and the team doctor on the other. Pereira turned the car down the main road into Lisbon.

Cristiano lay face up on the flat platform of the imaging machine, a small pillow under his head.

'Okay, you are allowed to breathe, but please try to remain perfectly still,' the technician said, placing a set of headphones over his ears.

'I hope this is Brazilian music,' he said, tapping the headphones.

The technician smiled. 'Stay perfectly still.' He stepped back, went to the control panel, and punched some buttons. The machine whined to life and Cristiano, table and all, moved slowly into the imaging tunnel until only his feet were sticking out.

After the body scan, Cristiano was ushered into a small conference room, accompanied by Pereira, Pontes, and the team doctor. He sat down, picked up a magazine, and started reading it.

The cardiologist had some big MRI pictures up on a light box. 'Okay,' the doctor said to Pereira. 'It was good you brought him to us. See here?' He pointed to a dark place on the MRI. 'A defect. Probably from birth.'

Cristiano lowered the magazine.

Pereira stood up. 'Is it serious?'

'The heart is always serious business,' the cardiologist said. 'In this case, the defect is fixable. I'm going to schedule surgery.'

Cristiano sucked in a breath and felt his heart race even more than it usually did. He felt sick. 'Am I going to die?' he asked. 'I'm only fifteen!'

'Not today,' the cardiologist said. 'By the way, we get to shoot you with a laser.'

'You're not making me feel better,' Cristiano said.

'Will he be able to play?' Pereira asked.

The cardiologist took a long time to answer. 'Honestly, I don't know.'

CHAPTER 15

The laser surgery on Cristiano's damaged heart was a success and he was back on the pitch in less than a week, much to Cristiano's relief. What looked like a bad start to the new century turned out to be a blessing. Cristiano felt stronger and faster than he ever had before. It was as if he doubled his speed. And he never seemed to run out of energy.

The coaching staff sat in awe when he took to the pitch for the first game since his surgery.

'It's a miracle. Cristiano Ronaldo is a miracle!' Cardoso marvelled from his seat in the stands.

Augusto Inácio, the team manager, came into the stands with two other men, Jose Mourinho, the manager of Porto, and an assistant.

Even from out on the pitch, Cristiano recognized

Mourinho and his heart raced. Calm down, he thought to himself.

'Boy, they'll let anybody in here now,' Cardoso said and offered his hand to Mourinho when he sat down.

'I was just about to say the same thing,' Mourinho replied, smiling to his friend.

'What's the manager of Porto doing here?' Cardoso asked.

'I missed my mates,' Mourinho lied, turning his attention to the pitch. 'Truthfully? I'm here to look at your fifteen year old.'

Inácio sat down next to him. 'You must be talking about our Ronnie.'

Cristiano charged down the pitch faster than anyone had ever seen him before. Ricardo Quaresma, the seventeen-year-old forward, could not keep up with him.

'I swear he is faster than he was before the surgery,' Silva said. 'Is that possible?'

'Someone should give him a ticket for speeding,' Pereira said.

'If they could keep up, they would,' Silva said.

The coaches all laughed. Their wonder boy had returned to the pitch, better than ever.

Mourinho leaned close to his assistant and whispered in his ear, 'There goes Van Basten's son.'

'I heard that,' Inácio said, grinning. 'And you can't have him yet.'

'Who said anything about wanting anybody, Augusto? I am here to watch a match with my mates, that's all. Don't tell me you regret inviting me,' Mourinho kidded. 'Your Ronnie is one-of-a-kind. I see him on the first team in a year.'

'No matter how much *bacalhau* we feed him, he's still scrawny,' Inácio said. 'If he goes up against those U18 brutes and shows his stuff, they will eat him alive.'

'Then you need to make him strong,' Mourinho said.

Inácio took his friend Mourinho's advice and started the fifteen-year-old Cristiano on the U16 team, but within two weeks, he was already playing with the U17 team after showing his incredible individual skill over three games, scoring eight goals. The other teams were no match for his artistry on the pitch as he bobbed and weaved through the defenders, the ball glued to his foot. Inácio put him and the U17s up against the U18 squad and Cristiano's side won. The next day, he moved up again. The U18 team was up against the Sporting B-Side, which was composed of the senior team reserves.

Cristiano trotted to the touchline and took to the pitch.

The U18 striker couldn't believe it. 'Hey! Where do you think you're going, ET?' he asked.

Cristiano stopped, turned to face him, and grinned. He liked the new nickname. First Little Bee, then Cry Baby, then Ronnie, and now ET. They called him ET because they thought he was out of this world. The name made him happy.

'Your team is over there,' the striker said, pointing to the other pitch where the younger team was playing a match.

'Didn't anybody tell you? I'm your new winger.' He flashed a grin and took to the pitch. And led the team to victory, scoring two in an incredible performance, leaving no doubt in anyone's mind that there was only one place left for him to go.

A month later, Cristiano lay on his bunk playing FIFA when a team clerk came in and dropped a large yellow envelope on his chest. 'Payday,' he said without any more explanation and left.

Cristiano quickly ripped it open and a huge pile of Escudo notes dropped out. More than he expected. He thumbed through them, counting.

He trotted along the path to the administrative offices, knocked on the accountant's door, and went in. The team accountant was behind her desk typing lightning fast on a large calculator. 'Help you?' she asked.

Cristiano waved the money. 'There's over 280 Euros here!'

She lowered her half glasses down her nose and sighed. 'Name?'

'Cristiano Ronaldo,' he said. 'But you can call me *ET.*'

'Oh yes,' she said, as if she had heard his name a thousand times. She opened up a big book, flipped through the pages, and stopped when she found his name. 'That is the correct amount,' she said. 'Are you saying I shorted you?'

'No,' he said. 'I'm saying you gave me more than I am owed.'

'Well, that's a refreshing first,' she said. 'Look, this is your final payment. Did you or did you not play for U16, U17, and U18 this year?'

'Final payment?' Cristiano asked and started to shake. 'I don't understand!'

Augusto Inácio and his co-manager Manuel Fernandes came into the office and went over to the accountant. 'I hear Ronnie is trying to give our money back?' he said, more for Cristiano's benefit. They had been lurking just outside the office and heard everything.

'Yes, it seems he thinks we pay him too much,' the accountant replied.

'No sir, I am not, I was just curious why I had—'

'You have an agent, correct?'

'Yes sir, but what does that have to do with—?'

'Not anymore.'

Cristiano felt like he just got hit from behind. He had a sinking feeling and felt the blood rush from his face. He thought his bad luck was behind him. And now this. No more Sporting. No more agent. 'A-am I fired, sir?'

Inácio looked up from the file drawer he was thumbing through and thought about it for a moment; then both he and Fernandes burst out laughing. 'Fired? Yes, I'm firing you. *Upward* – to the first team!' They laughed some more and it took a moment for Cristiano to grasp what was happening to him.

'First team?'

'And we think you need a new agent. I've already called Jorge Mendes.'

Cristiano held his breath. He had heard of Mendes. He was one of the best agents in the business.

'I can't very well negotiate a contract with *you,* can I? You might sell yourself short,' Inácio said.

'I would never sell myself short,' Cristiano boasted.

'Really? Then why did you come here to complain that we gave you too much money?'

'I didn't! I just—.' He cut himself off and grinned broadly.

'You are one of the most mature sixteen-year-olds I have ever had the pleasure of working with. And I look forward to more years with you on the first team. Congratulations, Ronnie,' he said and shoved out his hand.

Cristiano shook the team manager's hand, first slowly, then enthusiastically. Then he lost it, reeled Inácio in, and hugged him like one of his teammates. He tried to compose himself and looked into Inácio's eyes, holding back the tears.

Inácio could see the boy was struggling. 'That's right. They call you *Cry Baby.*'

'They *do?!*' Cristiano said in mock surprise. But he couldn't keep a straight face and burst out laughing. His laughter was infectious and Inácio, Fernandes, and the accountant joined in.

Cristiano hired superstar agent Jorge Mendes to guide the next phase of his career – which included moving out of the dorm room and into his own apartment in Lisbon. In August 2001, Cristiano signed his first professional contract – a four-year exclusive deal with Sporting Lisbon for 2,000 Euros a month and a 20 million-Euro buyout.

From now on, everything in his life changed at a rapid pace.

The first thing he did when he got a chunk of money was send it home. His brother, Hugo, had gone through rehab, but it had not worked. Cristiano was worried sick about him. The doctors in Madeira recommended another rehab session. This time, Cristiano paid for it. His father had checked into rehab too, for his drinking. Cristiano prayed it would work.

CHAPTER 16

Cristiano was excited about the friendly game between Sporting and Manchester United. The Red Devils had come to Lisbon to inaugurate the new state-of-the-art *Estadio Jose Alvalade XXI* stadium in the summer of 2003. Cristiano's friend had told him there were scouts everywhere, and they were all watching him.

Carlos Queiroz, who was a Sporting coach in the nineties, was now Sir Alex Ferguson's assistant coach at Manchester United, and kept pace with his boss. They had been scouting Ronaldo for the last couple of years after he had come to their attention. This was their first chance to get a good look at the kid in a big game.

'Okay, everybody – listen!' Cristiano shouted and his voice echoed off the dressing room walls.

The rest of his teammates stopped what they were doing.

'What are we listening for, Ronnie?' João Pinto asked.

Outside, the sounds of the crowd grew louder and louder.

'You hear that?'

'Yes. Fans.'

'Fifty-two *thousand* fans,' Cristiano said.

'Yeah,' Luis Filipe said. 'So what?'

'All here to see me,' Cristiano said boldly, puffing out his chest.

'Oh man! Get this guy now!' Lourenço said. He ran over, pulled Cristiano to the floor and dove on him. 'Get him! Before he starts crying!'

Cristiano laughed and tried to twist away from them, but more guys piled on top of him and he couldn't move.

'Take it back!' Pinto said.

'Okay, okay,' Cristiano said, fighting and laughing. 'I take it back! I take it back!'

The guys got off him and Pinto helped him to his feet. 'You need to respect your elders,' he kidded.

'Okay, I admit it – some of the fans are yours,' Cristiano said. Everyone laughed.

Their new manager, Fernando Santos, came into the room. It was almost game time. 'All right. I have some good news and some bad news. The bad news is Ferguson thinks we are a bunch of *chorãos.*'

They laughed. Ferguson thought they were a bunch of wimps.

'What's the good news?' Cristiano asked.

'The good news is we are going to win!' Santos said.

It was a few minutes to game time. Cristiano knew his folks were in the stands and his heart raced.

Dolores and Jose Dinis had VIP seats in the owner's box. Jose Dinis had finished rehab and stopped drinking, but today he did not feel well and Dolores wanted him to rest in the hotel room. He insisted on coming to see his son play. She kept an eye on him. She knew him too well. If something really bothered him, he would try to hide it from her. The doctors said his kidneys and his liver were in bad shape and he was hoping they were wrong. She knew better.

'You're going to the doctor,' she said.

'*After* the game,' Jose Dinis insisted.

The match started and the game got off to a slow start. After fifteen minutes, midfielder Fabio Rochemback took a free kick from a promising position and just missed, putting it over the crossbar. Fabien Barthez, the legendary Manchester United goalkeeper, flashed him a big smile. A few minutes later, Cristiano fired at Barthez's goal but the Frenchman sent the ball careering elsewhere. That was the story of the game for Cristiano. He drove John O'Shea, the United midfielder who was marking him, nuts on the pitch, but he couldn't finish. Finally Rio Jorge blasted the ball to Filipe and he squeaked the ball past Barthez, scoring the first goal for Sporting. The 50,000 fans in the *Alvalade* went wild.

Sir Alex Ferguson sat on the visitor bench and never took his eyes off Cristiano. The kid showed a lot of talent. Ferguson loved his technical skills, his pace, and his swift shots at goal.

Ferguson looked at his Portuguese assistant coach, nodded, and Queiroz knew he had made his decision.

At the half-time break, the Man U General Manager, Peter Kenyon, hurried down the rows of the stands and walked over to Sir Alex Ferguson. 'I already know what you're going to say, Fergie,' he said.

'We are not leaving this stadium without signing that boy,' Ferguson said. 'Was that it?'

Kenyon looked across the pitch at the Sporting Lisbon dugout – and nodded. 'Word-for-word.'

Sporting took to the pitch for the second half in their black and white away uniforms to confuse Man U and catch them off-guard. It worked. Pinto scored two more goals, one with an assist from Cristiano to end the game 3-1.

On the plane back to the UK, Ferguson walked down the aisle and stopped in front of John O'Shea's seat. 'Need something for that migraine the young lad Ronaldo gave you today, John?'

'As a matter of fact, sir, I know the cure,' John O'Shea said. 'We took a vote, sir.' He waved his arm around the plane at the other team members.

'You voted?' Ferguson was amused. What could they possibly be voting on? 'This isn't a democracy, John. I'm the boss here.'

'We want Cristiano Ronaldo on the team.'

Ferguson looked around the plane cabin and when his eyes met Carlos Queiroz's, they shared a smile. The decision made – and set in stone. But the team did not know that yet.

Every member of the squad agreed with O'Shea.

'You're kidding, right? He didn't score a single goal,' Ferguson said.

'With all due respect, sir,' Fabien Barthez said. 'What game were you watching?'

Ferguson studied his men, amused. 'I'm glad we all agree. How would it look to bring the kid to Manchester only to have you loathe him?'

When the team realized what Sir Alex was saying, they cheered and when Sir Alex walked back to his seat, he paused as he passed Queiroz's seat and whispered, 'Mission accomplished.'

After the game that day, Ferguson and Peter

Kenyon had had a private chat with Cristiano and his new agent, and the next day they flew him on a private jet to Manchester, England. Sporting agreed to sell him to Manchester United for more than twelve million pounds.

CHAPTER 17

Cristiano stepped into Sir Alex Ferguson's office at Old Trafford in Manchester, England. Carlos Queiroz accompanied him so he could translate for him. The teenager from Madeira did not speak English. Sir Alex stared out the window at the pitch where a squad was training.

'You wanted to see me, sir?' Cristiano asked.

Sir Alex turned from the window and jerked a thumb back behind him. 'Best view in football, don't you think, Chris?' he asked.

Cristiano nodded. Here comes another nickname.

'We need a number for you, Chris,' Sir Alex said.

'Oh, number. Jersey number,' Cristiano said. 'Would it be okay if I used 28? That's my old number back at Sporting.'

Sir Alex smiled at him. 'We had a wee smaller

number in mind for you,' he said as he picked up a red jersey from his desk and tossed it at him. Cristiano caught it and unfurled it. It had his name in big bold white letters on the back and the number 7.

Cristiano caught his breath. 'Seven!' he said, a little too loud. 'But this is Beckham's number!'

'And Berry and Best and Coppell and Robson and Cantona,' Ferguson said, smiling at the teenager. 'And now it is yours. You're not refusing it, are you?' he kidded.

Cristiano blushed. 'No sir! I am not as crazy as everyone says I am!'

Sir Alex and Queiroz laughed.

'I just hope I can live up to it,' Cristiano said.

'You will,' Sir Alex said.

Three days later, Cristiano Ronaldo put on the red shirt for the first time and made his Manchester United debut on the bench against Bolton. He sat next to Eric Djemba-Djemba. 'Everything is happening fast for you?' Djemba-Djemba asked.

'Not fast *enough*,' Cristiano said, his eyes glued to the pitch, jumping out of his skin. Maybe they are testing my patience, he thought.

'You're up, Ronnie,' Queiroz said and Cristiano started to warm up.

At the sixtieth minute, Cristiano Ronaldo came in for Nicky Butt.

Sir Alex said, 'They're tired, son – go punch a hole in their defence.'

'Yes, sir!' Cristiano said.

Nicky Butt slapped Ronaldo's hand and the first Portuguese player in Man U's history took to the pitch at Old Trafford for the first time. The public address system announced his name and the crowd roared with delight.

Man U was up 1-0 and it was time to see if the world's most expensive teenager could help make their win inevitable.

Bolton was ruthless to Cristiano and went after him with a vengeance, but where the eighteen-year-old came from, in the streets of Madeira, getting beaten up was all part of the game.

Cristiano had an assist to Ryan Giggs for the second goal. Two more goals by Paul Scholes and Ruud van Nistelrooy gave the Red Devils a 4-0 win.

The fans went nuts. When Cristiano left the pitch, everyone was on their feet and the stands shook with excitement.

'It looks like the fans have a new hero,' Ferguson said and slapped Queiroz on the back.

Both men turned and followed the team off the pitch.

CHAPTER 18

Cristiano depended on Carlos Queiroz to translate for him, so he was disappointed when his coach came to break the news at his home in Alderly Edge.

'I won't be with you, Ronnie. I'm leaving Manchester,' Carlos Queiroz said.

'But – who will speak for me?' Cristiano pleaded.

'You will,' Queiroz said. 'It's time you learned English.'

Cristiano flashed a grin. 'Does this mean I'm allowed to make mistakes?'

He was kidding and Queiroz knew it and shook his head, chuckling. 'No. Francisco Filho will make sure you don't say the wrong thing to the boss.'

Filho was Brazilian and had been coaching the Man U youth teams since last year. He would help with the translation duties.

Cristiano knew he was going to miss his mentor. 'Filho is a good man, but he's not you,' Cristiano said.

'Look, I'm disappointed too. But it would have to be something very special for me to leave you now, you know that, right?'

'You better have a good reason,' Cristiano warned, half-smiling. 'Who am I going to cry to when they beat me up out there on the pitch?'

'I've seen you. I think you can handle yourself just fine. Aren't you going to ask me why I am leaving?'

'I already know. You're going to take over as manager of Real Madrid.' Then Cristiano was silent for a moment. It was as if serendipity had suddenly dropped from the sky and brought his life into focus. 'Did I ever tell you my dream? I've had it since I was a little boy!'

'No, but I'm guessing you're going to tell me now,' Queiroz said dryly.

'I want to play for Real Madrid!'

Queiroz grinned. 'Who doesn't?'

Cristiano laughed. That was what his godfather

always said. He smiled at his coach. 'Don't forget about me, Coach,' he said.

Queiroz stopped and studied the boy. 'How could I?'

He loved him like a son and bringing him here to United was his idea. Now Cristiano's career was just beginning and he wouldn't be here to see it.

'Learn English!' he said, pointing at him.

Cristiano smiled and hugged him. Queiroz left Manchester a few days later for Real Madrid, but it wouldn't be long before their paths crossed again.

The next day, Luis Felipe Scolari, also known as Big Phil, of the Portuguese National Team, called Cristiano. Big Phil invited him to play in an international friendly against Kazakhstan. Jorge Mendes, his agent, was already on his way over with plane tickets to Chaves, Portugal, where the team had a training camp.

When Sir Alex Ferguson heard that Big Phil, who had won the World Cup with Brazil in 2002, was about to spirit his new prodigy away for the weekend, he snatched up the phone and made the call. 'You know I am pacing Cristiano, so I want you to swear you won't overuse him.'

'Would I do that, Fergie?' Scolari kidded.

'I'm not kidding, Phil,' Sir Alex said. 'I have big plans for him… don't mess them up.' Sir Alex hung up the phone.

Three days later, Luis Figo and Rui Costa, world class stars and the leaders of the national team, took Cristiano aside in the dressing room before the game. He couldn't believe it. Here were his heroes giving him advice before a game. 'Stay calm,' Figo said. 'Play the way you always do.'

'Don't let your emotions get the better of you,' Rui Costa instructed.

At half time, Cristiano knew he was going to get on the pitch. Scolari gave the signal and the winger he was subbing for trotted off the pitch and ran right for him. Cristiano held his breath as Luis Figo hugged him. 'Stay calm,' he whispered and slapped his hand, then hurried over to the bench to watch the rest of the game. Dolores saw it all. Her son. Figo. She was incredibly proud. Jose Dinis was speechless.

Cristiano looked at his hand – the one that Figo shook – and smiled. 'This hand just touched greatness!' he said, then charged off onto the pitch to take his position as winger for the Portuguese National team.

Later that night, as Cristiano stood outside the team hotel waiting for a car to take him to the airport to fly back to Manchester, Scolari came out of the hotel lobby waving a newspaper. 'Check this out!' he said, handing him the paper.

Cristiano looked at the paper and opened to the sports page. They named him 'Player of the Game.' He looked up and grinned, happier than he had ever been.

'Congratulations!' Scolari said.

A town car pulled up and the driver got out and opened the door for him. Cristiano got in and Scolari leaned in after him. 'Make sure you tell Fergie I didn't overwork you.'

'Yes sir,' Cristiano said and Scolari closed the door.

After Cristiano returned to England, he played in thirty-nine more games that season, scored eight goals, and led Manchester United to win the FA Cup for the first time in four years. It was 22 May 2004.

'You can be a lot better,' his boss had told him. 'And you will.'

CHAPTER 19

Cristiano stared at the ceiling of his hotel room in Moscow. It was September of 2005 and almost game time. He sat up, clicked the remote, and turned on the TV. Everything was in Russian. He had no idea what they were talking about. He leaned over the side of the bed, rummaged through his Portuguese National kit bag, and finally found what he was looking for: a packaged biscuit. He unwrapped it and ate it ravenously. The game against Russia was a couple of hours away. It was crucial in the team's quest for the 2006 World Cup.

The phone rang and he almost jumped a mile.

'Ronnie, I need you to come to my room.' It was Scolari and he sounded scared.

Cristiano hurriedly pulled on a pair of trousers

and shirt, slipped into some shoes, and rushed down the hall to Big Phil's room, a few doors down. When he knocked on the door, Luis Figo answered and let him in. That was odd. Rui Costa was there too.

'Now we're meeting in Russian hotel rooms?' he joked.

No one in the room was laughing.

'Ron, it's your father,' Scolari said.

Cristiano felt a great weight slam against his chest. He knew this might happen; they had warned him ever since July when he had flown his dad to London and put him in the hospital. Please, not now, he thought. I'm not ready. 'He's still in the hospital in London, right?' he asked, steadying himself on a chair.

'He passed away a few minutes ago,' Scolari said. 'I just spoke with the doctor.'

Cristiano felt as if all the life had drained out of him. 'H-how can that be? I just talked to him this morning,' Cristiano said.

'He fought hard, but his battle is over and he is out of pain.' This was hard for Scolari to say, and Figo draped an arm over his shoulder to support him.

'He lost the war, Ronnie, I'm so sorry,' Figo said. 'He is in God's hands now.'

Scolari studied him for a moment. 'I never shared this before but – I lost my father too. I know what it feels like.' He held his arms open and Cristiano folded into them and sobbed. 'We will fly you to London,' Scolari said. 'To be with your family.'

Cristiano thought about it and shook his head. 'No,' he said. 'I want to play the game, in honour of my father. I wouldn't be here if it wasn't for him.' And Cristiano Ronaldo kept his promise.

Three days later, Cristiano boarded a private jet for Madeira. The blue waters of the Atlantic were a mirror and he could see the clouds in it. His thoughts drifted to his father. He hoped he wasn't scared when he passed. Cristiano knew he would never get over the loss, but he prayed he would get used to it. His father had died from alcoholism and that reminded him of the promise he had made to himself when he was just a young boy – to never drink. He was true to his word.

The private jet touched down at Funchal Airport and Cristiano stepped off and immediately got into a limousine that took him to the chapel at the Santo Antonio cemetery. As the long car drove up the road to Santo Antonio, he saw the streets lined with thousands of his fans, hoping to get a look at their homegrown superstar. When the car pulled into the car park, Cristiano saw the priest standing outside, flanked by Fernão de Sousa, his godfather, and Jaime Fernandes, his father's best friend. Hundreds of people were inside, including Scolari. The service was about to begin. They were waiting for his arrival.

His father's coffin was at the front.

The pastor delivered a brief sermon. Cristiano was brokenhearted. He remembered when his father teased him for losing his football when it rolled down the hill and then gave him a new one just before Christmas. It was the best Christmas present he had ever received. He could see some of his friends from the street sitting around in the pews of the chapel and thought about how they kept him from playing because he was too young. He remembered his father telling him how he was late to his christening because of an Andorinha match and how his tardiness just about drove the priest crazy. His father was there for him when Nacional and Sporting and Manchester United all came calling. He tried so hard to help his father, to give back, but in the end, he could not. There were things that even money could not buy.

After the service, the family buried Jose Dinis dos Santos Aveiro in the Santo Antonio cemetery. His white gravestone read in Portuguese, *His wife, sons, sons-in-law, daughters, grandchildren, mother and other family members will miss him forever.*

For Cristiano, it meant he would not only miss his father forever, he would also keep searching for him. It was an old Portuguese tradition.

Cristiano went home to Manchester and played for the Red Devils for five more seasons, totaling 118 goals in 292 appearances. His family was always near him. 'If my family isn't okay,' he said, 'then I don't feel right.'

In 2008, Cristiano helped his team win the Premiership and Champions League trophies and then personally won football's most prestigious prize given to an individual, the Ballon d'Or. He was crowned the greatest player in the world.

When Cristiano accepted the trophy, Sir Alex Ferguson surprised him and mounted the stage to say a few words about his prodigy. 'Cristiano deserves this award and the club is thrilled with this latest success. Manchester United has been waiting for this moment for forty years,' he said. The crowd cheered and Sir Alex looked over at Cristiano and smiled. He could tell the twenty-four-year-old was holding back the tears. But he wasn't finished yet. 'One of Cristiano's lesser-known virtues,' he continued, 'is his courage and bravery. Courage in football, as in life, manifests itself in different ways. But the courage to move forward, no matter how many times he is kicked, that is the courage that Cristiano Ronaldo knows all too well. Very few players have that level of courage. Some believe the greatest courage in football is the courage to win the ball. The other kind of courage – and it's a moral courage – is the courage to keep the ball. That is what Ronaldo has. All the great players have it.'

Despite his triumphs, at the end of the fifth season at Manchester United, in 2008, Cristiano Ronaldo wanted to move to Real Madrid.

CHAPTER 20

When Carlos Queiroz called him from his home in Portugal, Sir Alex knew it was serious because his former assistant manager liked to talk face-to-face. 'Cristiano is here now. I need you,' he said.

It took Sir Alex a couple of hours to get to Chester Airport and board a direct flight to Portugal. When he knocked on Carlos Queiroz's front door, Cristiano Ronaldo opened it, and he was surprised. 'Sir Alex!' he said, standing there.

'Well, Chris? Are you going to invite me in?' asked Sir Alex.

Cristiano blushed. 'Oh! Sorry, boss!' he said and stepped aside.

Sir Alex came into the room and looked around. Queiroz, who was in the kitchen, came in with a big smile on his face. 'Fergie! How nice of you to come.'

Cristiano looked at Queiroz, then back to Sir Alex. 'I only told Carlos about Real Madrid three hours ago. What took you?' he kidded.

'I would have been here sooner, but they still don't have time travel from the UK,' Sir Alex said, sitting down. 'Now tell me all about what Calderon told you.'

They all sat down and it did not take long for Cristiano to tell him how Ramon Calderon, the president of Real Madrid, offered a lot of money to bring Cristiano to the team – now.

Sir Alex studied his prodigy for a moment. 'I know you want to go and I know it has been your lifelong dream to play for Real. And we are grateful we had you for the past five seasons.'

'Sir, I am the player I am because of United,' Cristiano said. 'I am eternally grateful to you. I want to do the right thing by you.'

'Yes, it's true, we made you the player you are today. But that's only one side of the story,' Sir Alex said. 'You brought excitement back to the team at a time when we needed it most. You brought self-expression, something that had been missing for

quite a few seasons. I know why Calderon wants
you. I know he's been broadcasting it to the world
that you will soon be playing for Real Madrid. They
want to pay you more money than anyone has
ever paid for a player because they want to make
a statement: that Real Madrid is the best in the
world. But it will all be on his terms. If I do that,
my honour is gone, everything is gone for me, and I
don't care if you have to sit in the stands. I know it
won't come to that, but I just have to tell you I will
not let you leave this year. Do you understand what
I mean? It's about respect.'

Cristiano nodded. 'Yes sir, I know exactly what
you mean.' He could feel his emotions welling up
inside him.

'I know how badly you want to go to Real. But
the way Calderon did this – I'd rather shoot you
than sell you to him.'

Cristiano looked at his manager – the best coach
in the world. He knew how blunt Sir Alex could
be, and at that moment, he realized he would have
to give up his dream for a little while longer. He
laughed. 'I'm not laughing because I think you're

kidding,' he said. 'I'm laughing because I know you're not.' He took a deep breath. 'Boss, I want to tell you that what you did for me is unbelievable and I'll never forget it for the rest of my life. When I arrived at Manchester as an eighteen year old, you were like a father to me in football. You gave me opportunities and taught me many things. I remember when I first arrived in the club, I asked for the number 28 shirt, and you gave me the number 7. It put me under a lot of pressure but you told me it wouldn't be a problem and that I would deserve to wear this shirt because I was a fantastic player. You taught me how to be a good professional and a good young man, and you are a fantastic man and person. You will always be number one in my book.'

Sir Alex looked at Cristiano, and softened a bit. 'I want you to know, Cristiano, you are the most gifted player I have ever managed,' he said. 'You have surpassed all the other great ones I have coached at United – and I have had many.'

They hugged and then Sir Alex left Portugal and returned to Manchester.

When Sir Alex Ferguson and Carlos Queiroz decided to work on bringing Cristiano Ronaldo to Manchester United all those years ago, the great manager asked his coach and friend, 'How long do you think we can keep him before someone else spirits him away?'

Carlos Queiroz said, 'If you get five years out of him, you've struck gold.'

Sir Alex got six.

Cristiano Ronaldo kept his word and played for a sixth season at Manchester United, then moved to Real Madrid when Florentino Perez, the new Real Madrid president, offered him more money than any single football player had ever been paid in the history of the game.

CHAPTER 21

Cristiano smiled. He smiled a lot these days. He took one more look around the Bernabéu, and then he stepped out onto the green walkway that meandered over the pitch and led to the stage. More than 82,000 fans had come to catch a glimpse of the kid from Madeira who had made a name for himself – from the streets of Santo Antonio to the pitch of Manchester United – and along the way became the greatest player in the world. Now he belonged to Real Madrid.

Florentino Perez, the president of Real Madrid, was at the podium when Cristiano bounded on to the stage and greeted him. He embraced his heroes, Alfredo Di Stefano and Eusébio, then stood quietly as Perez introduced them all.

'Thank you all for being here,' the president of

Real Madrid began. 'You represent the greatest symbol of Madridismo – the passion of the Club Members and how the fans all around the world feel about this team. You are essential in making this the most admired and respected club in the world. What is happening tonight has no precedent and your overwhelming attendance here represents the essence of Real Madrid.'

The crowd cheered wildly.

'Thank you for being the real stars in this unstop-pable showcasing of strength, excitement, and vision. There are Portuguese fans here with us today to help us greet one of their own into our house. It is an honour for us to have with us one of the greatest players of all time, and a symbol of what is great about Portuguese football – the legendary Eusébio!'

The crowd was on their feet for the Portuguese legend and Cristiano watched him take a bow.

'In that case,' Perez continued. 'You must also be aware that we have on this stage for the first time at the same time, two friends who are the greatest players in history – Eusébio and Di Stefano.'

Eusébio and Di Stefano draped their arms over each other's shoulders and greeted the crowd.

When the cheering died down, Perez continued. 'Very few people in the world ever reach this kind of greatness. Today, we have one who has. Real Madrid welcomes one of the chosen ones – capable of making the dreams of football fans throughout the world come true. Please, everyone, welcome Cristiano Ronaldo!'

Cristiano turned around and waved to the crowd all around him. They returned the gesture by shouting, 'Si si si si Ronaldo en el Madrid!' He loved that he shared their same amazement. For him, Real Madrid was always the dream and now it was real.

After Perez finished his speech, he turned the podium over to Cristiano and the boy from Madeira knew exactly what he was going to say. He would speak the truth. Just like his mother and father had taught him. 'I am very happy to be here,' he said and the crowd went insane. It was more than a minute before he could continue. 'This is a dream come true,' he said. 'As a child I dreamed of playing for

Real Madrid.' He heard his own words and when the crowd roared he had to catch his breath. 'I didn't expect there to be so many of you!' he said and the crowd laughed. 'This is unbelievable,' he said. 'Thank you all.' Then he recalled the popular Real Madrid cheer, took a deep breath, and shouted, 'Hala Madrid!'

The crowd was on their feet and it was all for him. He could not see them but he knew his mother, Hugo, Elma, and Katia were there. He knew his godfather, Fernão de Sousa, was out there and so were his friends from Santo Antonio. They were all there. He longed for his father to hold him one more time and searched for him in the crowd. He thought of his father, gone just a few years. He realized he had gotten used to him being gone, but he would never get over it. Forever longing, always seeking. Then someone tossed him a ball and he did a stepover and launched it and caught it on the top of his head, just like he practised thousands of times on Rua Quinta Falcão in his beloved Madeira, where everyone talked funny.

CRISTIANO RONALDO

The crowd was loud and happy and full of love.

It was magic to him and he was the happiest man on earth.

THE WORLD'S #1 BEST-SELLING FOOTBALL SERIES!

THE FLEA

The Amazing Story of Leo
Messi

Michael Part

Cristiano
Ronaldo
The Rise of a Winner

Michael Part

Neymar
The Wizard

Michael Part

Luis
Suarez
A Striker's Story

Michael Part

James
The Incredible
Number 10

Michael Part

Balotelli
The Untold
Story

Michael Part

Learn more at www.solebooks.com

Printed in Germany
by Amazon Distribution
GmbH, Leipzig